INCREDIBLE
BASEBALL STATS

The Coolest, Strangest Stats and Facts in Baseball History

BY KEVIN REAVY AND RYAN SPAEDER
FOREWORD BY WADE BOGGS

SPORTS
PUBLISHING

Visit our website at www.sportspubbooks.com.

10 9 8 7 6 5 4 3

Library of Congress Cataloging-in-Publication Data is available on file.

Cover design by Tom Lau
Cover photo credit iStockphoto

ISBN: 978-1-61321-894-5
Ebook ISBN: 978-1-61321-895-2
Printed in the United States of America

TABLE OF CONTENTS

II. NATIONAL LEAGUE   123

In Memoriam of the lone major leaguers who lost their lives serving in World War II, both Hall of Famers in our book:
1st Lt Harry O'Neill (USMC), KIA March 6, 1945
Capt Elmer Gedeon (USAAF), KIA April 20, 1944

ACKNOWLEDGMENTS

Writing this book required the help, encouragement, and support of some really great people:

Sean Forman and Baseball-Reference.com, for helping casual fans and professional researchers alike see through the statistical looking glass of baseball's rich history. The Baseball-Reference play index really helps make this book possible.

Michael Kirk, for his mastery in finding, fixing, and fact-checking numerous aspects of this book along the way.

Julie Ganz, for what was surely an arduous task editing this book and directing our progress. We didn't make it easy, but she's always a pleasure to work with.

Wade Boggs, for his generosity, and tremendous foreword.

Amy McCormick, for her great work on the glossary and Rob Campbell for bringing two baseball nerds together to make this happen.

Also, a huge thank-you to the following for their invaluable assistance for this book and over the years:

Lyle "Chip" Chipperson, Kevin Durso, Peter Gammons, Dan Hirsch, Christopher Kamka, Jonah Keri, Frank Klose, Andrew Owens, Tim Raines, Matt Rappa, Mark Simon, Jayson Stark, Brian Startare, Ben Steffen, Lyndsay Taylor, Daren Willman, Nolan Ryan's fastball, and the National Baseball Hall of Fame and Museum.

A note from Kevin: I would like to thank my family— Charlotte, Ed, Dave, Colleen, et al. They're the best. Also, a big thank-you to my friends—Mike, Fitz, Jim, Teal, Tiff, Brad, Andrew, Aric, and Mary. They're ok. Finally, and most importantly, this book wouldn't be possible if I couldn't unwind after long writing sessions with wings and a pint at Frank's American Pub, the Chester County 'Cheers.'

A note from Ryan: Mom and Dad—thank you for backing me in everything I do and all of the decisions I make; I love you. Georgie, Jenna, Carlie (aka "Oh"), and Jake(man), your support drives me. Finally, thank you to the everyone who follows me on Twitter. Without you, I am just a crazy person spouting off statistical nonsense.

FOREWORD

Wade Boggs played the game the right way. His skillset was often underappreciated throughout his career, as he caught the reputation as a Punch and Judy singles hitter—but he was so much more than that.

Wins above replacement (WAR), which is relied upon heavily today to measure a player's overall contribution to his team, can only be applied to Wade's career in retrospect. But when looking back on his prime seasons through sabermetric glasses, we can deduce that he was one of baseball's most valuable players. He led American League position players in WAR in 1986, 1987, and 1988 and was second in 1983, 1985, and 1989. Despite this, he never received a single first-place MVP vote.

Sabermetrics aside, Boggs was a decisive table setter for the Red Sox throughout his Boston tenure (1982–92), during which he maintained an on-base percentage of .428—besting the American League's cumulative OBP by 100 points (.328). He reached base a major-league–best 3,124 times during that same period—381 more than future Hall of Famer Tim Raines, who was second—and garnering a mere 470 strikeouts, which ranked 158th most.

Boggs's ability to get on base was emphasized by his ability to hit for a high average. In fact, in just his 58th career MLB at-bat (65th overall plate appearance), he singled to center field off the Tigers' Milt Wilcox, raising his lifetime batting average to .328—a clip he'd never drop below, all the way through to his final big league appearance with Tampa Bay on August 27, 1999.

Unlike Boston's greatest folk hero, Ted Williams, Boggs never batted .400 in a season; however, during his 162-game peak—from June 9, 1985 to June 6, 1986—he maintained a splendid .401 batting average.

Batting average—long used as the key measurement of a player's success at the plate—is now merely a supporting statistic. Boggs played ahead of his time; he knew that getting on base was what mattered most. His new-school approach yielded a .415 on-base percentage, 16th best in baseball history among players with at least 7,000 plate appearances. That's not to say that Boggs's "classic" stats aren't equally as impressive; he would have to return to baseball and go 0-for-854 for his career batting average to officially dip below .300.

This year, the Boston Red Sox decided to retire my #26 jersey. What an honor, to have my number up there in right field at Fenway Park with some of the greatest to ever wear the uniform!

It's another tremendously satisfying reward for all the hard work and dedication I put into the game throughout my life. I like to think I played the game the *right way.*

Pete Rose was one of my favorite players growing up, and very well might be the poster boy for leaving it all out on the field. That "Charlie Hustle" persona rubbed off on me, and is everything I preach to the kids I coach at Wharton High School in Florida. Maximum effort and hustle on every play are two things that require zero athletic ability. That's the kind of ballplayer I've enjoyed watching, and that's something I hope to instill in the next generation of players, from Little League on up.

When I played, I always had a plan and tried my best. Statistics weren't at the forefront of my mind, but I knew the stats would be there, if I did my job. Now, more than ever, baseball stats are celebrated and studied in a way that I think really honors the nuances of the game, and the little things that players, past and present, contribute to win games, and ultimately, the World Series.

I wish we had been able to bring home a World Series trophy for Boston during my tenure. Winning one with the Yankees in 1996 probably lost me a few fans, but I truly never wanted to leave Boston in the first place. Jean Yawkey, Sox owner during my career, had hopes that I'd retire a Red Sox, with the likes of Ted Williams and Carl Yastrzemski, and I was thrilled at the thought. Sadly, Mrs. Yawkey, my biggest fan, passed away in 1992, and the front office simply didn't offer me a contract when I was granted free agency shortly thereafter. But I'm proud of what I accomplished in Boston . . . and the same goes for New York, and Tampa Bay, where I still live.

Moneyball, and Billy Beane's philosophies chronicled within, really ushered in a newfound respect for the art of getting on base by any means necessary. I was "Billy Ball" before "Billy Ball." I had a job to do—setting the table for my teammates to knock in some runs. And getting on base 300 times a year was my goal, and my job. Today, that style is celebrated probably more than ever.

Mike Trout, for instance. He's an outstanding example of a player that plays hard and does all the little things on the stat sheet to help his team win. And fans really understand and appreciate everything he does. He's doing a heck of a job against pitchers today that seem to throw harder than ever before. Facing a guy like Aroldis Chapman, who throws impossible heat, has to be nerve-racking, but I'm sure he loves the challenge. I would revel in it.

That's the thing I miss most about playing—the one-on-one battle. That adrenaline rush in the batter's box was my favorite thing, and it's something I just can't get from watching on TV or in the stands. But, it's still exciting to see it in others. Unlike any other competition, there's a chance for history to be made every single day in baseball. The competition, and the history of it all, hooked me when I was young, and it's something that continues to drive my love of the game today.

This book celebrates a lot of that history. There are great stories in here, past and present, all told from a statistical standpoint—a fresh point of view on some of the best players and moments in baseball history. There is no stat for hustle and effort, but I'm sure either Ryan Spaeder or Kevin Reavy is somewhere in a lab right now testing out equations and theories to cook one up!

Baseball is a cool, fun game, in which a lot of cool, fun things have happened. You'll read a lot of that stuff in this book. The authors are big-time baseball fans, and that's the audience I played to. You guys—the fans—made my career.

My hope is that you'll find this plays to you as well. The authors' sole intentions were to put together a fun read, celebrating baseball's history and traditions through stats, and I think they did it the *right way*.

–**Wade Boggs**

Wade Boggs, warming up at Baltimore's Memorial Stadium in 1988. (Ted Straub)

INTRODUCTION

Baseball can be romanticized in any number of ways. As America's pastime and sporting tradition since the mid-1800s, the game offers sights, sounds, and smells that are deeply entrenched in our culture and personal lives.

For some, the experience may be less visceral.

Just as a computer programmer lives and breathes the binary 1s and 0s, and *http gigabyte gobbledygook* that operate in anonymity within a quarter-inch thick tablet computer, we obsess over baseball statistics. Stats give the game historical context, and measurables for past, present, and predictive analysis. The numbers may not always be what we see and experience at the ballpark, or through our television screen, but one thing is certainly true: Stats tell stories.

In 2000, Pedro Martinez tied for just the eighth-highest win total in baseball. Dig deeper and the numbers tell us that, if Martinez had been charged a run for every time he walked or hit a batter on the season (46 times total), he would still have the lowest ERA in the league.

Sure, Houston Astros second baseman Jose Altuve won the batting title in 2014. But did you know, at five-foot-five he was the shortest player with 225 hits in a season since Willie Keeler in 1897? That's a fun story.

Those are the kinds of stories we tell in this book —through stats.

America's fascination with baseball stats gave birth to fantasy sports, exciting home run chases, and thrilling pilgrimages to Cooperstown, New York, to visit the Baseball Hall of Fame and Museum—a building built on the historical records and statistical achievements of the game's greatest. The numbers are a very critical part of the story.

We scoured the records for untold tales, and looked at familiar ones from new statistical contexts. There's a monstrous pile of data and satiating sabermetric goodies in this book, if that's what you're into. But also, there are some really incredible stories.

STATS INCREDIBLE!

Every team chapter in the book ends with a collection of some of our favorite stats pertaining to that team, labeled, "Stats Incredible!" You can shoot to those sections for quick-hit stats, or just dive into the whole thing.

Overall, you'll find a brief team history for each franchise, along with a few subsections, with stats on some of their greatest players, moments, and achievements.

If you see a stat you don't know or understand, don't freak out. Check the glossary of terms in the back of the book.

I. AMERICAN LEAGUE

AMERICAN LEAGUE EAST

BALTIMORE ORIOLES

Est. 1901

In 2015, Manny Machado became the youngest player to play every game in a season for the Orioles since Cal Ripken Jr. in 1983—Ripken's first full season during his "Iron Man Streak."

The Baltimore Orioles are a storied franchise, but a complicated one. The original eight American League teams in 1901 featured a Baltimore Orioles, but not *the* Baltimore Orioles we know today. The modern O's squad is a descendant of the original Milwaukee Brewers of 1901, but not *the* Milwaukee Brewers we know today. Get it?

Deep breath . . .

The O's of today began as the Milwaukee Brewers in the American League's eight-team formation in 1901. One of the other eight was the Baltimore Orioles, but that franchise folded and opened up a spot for the New York Yankees in 1903. The Brewers moved from Milwaukee to Missouri in 1902 and became the St. Louis Browns. Fast forward fifty-two years, when the team was sold and moved to Baltimore, where the current Orioles started fresh and still reside. Ultimately, the team originally known as the Brewers became the Browns and finally the Orioles in less than fifty-five years.

The modern O's may prefer to promote their Hall of Fame Baltimore brethren of Cal Ripken Jr., Jim Palmer, Frank Robinson, et al, but that half-century in St. Louis is impossible to ignore.

St. Louis Browns

Third baseman Scott Rolen, upon being traded to the St. Louis Cardinals in 2002, remarked that he felt as though he had "died and gone to baseball heaven." Surely, the city today regards its lone baseball team as divine, stuffing the Busch Stadium cathedral to capacity with regularity. But perhaps the greatest example of St. Louis's reputation as an historically great baseball town is how the fans wrapped their arms around the Browns—an historically dreadful franchise.

After their first season in Missouri in 1902, the Browns finished second in the eight-team American League (78-58), but would fail to finish higher than fourth for the following 18 seasons. The NL Cardinals were having a rough couple of decades themselves, with just two third-place finishes over the same span. The early part of baseball's modern era would seem to paint a particularly hellish picture of the situation in St. Louis, but the fans persevered.

The 1915 St. Louis Browns, managed by Dodgers front-office legend, Branch Rickey (suited). (Author unknown; PD)

One of the few true gems of the Browns franchise was first baseman George Sisler, who ranks among the greatest pure hitters in baseball history, and was a true one-man show for the club.

In 1920, Sisler had 240 runs produced, accounting for 30.11% of his team's scoring that season—and the Browns finished third in the league in runs (797).

Sisler's greatest campaign was his 1922 MVP season, in which he led the league in batting average (.420), hits (246), runs (134), and stolen bases (51). He had more than twice as many games with three hits or more (36) as no-hit games (17). His .420 clip is good for third highest during the modern era of baseball (since 1901) and second highest during the Live Ball Era (since 1920) only to the .424 posted by his roommate at Sportsmans Park, Cards great Rogers Hornsby, in 1924.

Today, we wonder if there will ever be another .400 hitter. Tony Gwynn was the closest with the Padres in 1994 (.394). But from May 4, 1920 to April 17, 1924, spanning 425 games and parts of four MLB seasons, Sisler maintained a .402 average.

Zany owner Bill Veeck purchased the Browns in 1951 and immediately set his sights on making the Browns the top show in town, by any means necessary.

He famously signed Eddie Gaedel, a 3-foot-7 dwarf with the jersey number "1/8", and actually put him into a game to pinch hit. Gaedel's microscopic strike zone aided the inevitable walk, and pushed Major League Baseball toward a void of his contract the following day, instilling new discretionary disqualification rules based on height.

Veeck's fan-friendly style was a big hit. He signed former Cards greats to work for the team and generated a dizzying array of promotions to keep interest high. He even once allowed fans to pick a lineup and vote on managerial decisions during a game. It was all part of his master plan to drive the Cardinals out of town and lay sole claim to St. Louis and its fans.

And he would have gotten away with it too, if it wasn't for those meddling Brew makers . . .

Browns Out, Baltimore-Bound

In 1953, the Cardinals were sold to the local Anheuser-Busch brewery with the intent of staying put and having significant financial backing to do so.

Veeck could no longer compete, so he sold the stadium to the Cards and moved the team to Baltimore. Success would soon follow.

Since the move, Baltimore did what the Browns couldn't in St. Louis—win the World Series. The Orioles won it all three times (1966, 1970, 1983), totaling exactly one more championship than the Philadelphia Phillies (established in 1883) have to date.

Jim Palmer, who tossed a Live Ball era record 11 shutouts in which he allowed three-or-fewer baserunners, played on all three of Baltimore's championship teams. The owner of three Cy Young Awards over the span of four seasons (1973–76), he might be one of the most underappreciated hurlers of all time.

He ruled the 1970s, leading the decade in both ERA (2.58) and wins (186). Over the past 100 seasons, no other American League pitcher has had more sub-2.50 ERA seasons than Palmer.

Palmer also led the famed 1971 rotation that featured four 20-game winners. With Dave McNally, Pat Dobson, and Mike Cuellar, the quartet totaled 81 wins and registered a 1.131 WHIP, the best in baseball's Live Ball Era (1920+).

Palmer was "the man" in the early years of Baltimore baseball, but the "Iron Man" would eventually unseat him as the face of the franchise.

Cal Ripken Jr.
Ripken was a revolutionary shortstop, bringing unheard of offensive production to a predominantly defensive position.

Cal Ripken Sr. & Jr. during Junior's 1982 Rookie of the Year season.
(Baltimore Orioles / MLB)

He holds the AL record for All-Star appearances (19), making every squad from his second full season in the majors until his last. He has the most home runs (345) and RBIs (1,328) in history from the shortstop position, and is tied with Honus Wagner for most 10+ WAR seasons at shortstop (2). Overall, Ripken is one of just eleven players in history to have multiple 10+ WAR seasons, and Joe DiMaggio has zero.

While Derek Jeter gets a lot of credit these days as one of the greatest Yankees and maybe the best shortstop in the game's history, consider this:

In terms of WAR, one full season played by Ripken (162 games) is worth about 197 games played by Derek Jeter. While Jeter could return to baseball, go 0-for-1,376 and still not see his career batting average fall below Ripken's, overall game sways decidedly in Ripken's favor.

Ripken owns the fourth highest defensive WAR in baseball history (34.6), annihilating Jeter (-9.7), yet amazingly won just two Gold Glove awards to Jeter's five. One of Ripken's non-wins was one of the greatest fielding seasons of all time, as he committed just three errors in 680 chances, playing every game. But shortstops were supposed to be short, quick guys named "Pee Wee," and Ripken was tall, strong, and slowed by all that iron.

Famously, Ripken earned the "Iron Man" moniker, playing in 2,632 straight games. Only 34 players in the game's history have played 2,632 games *total*.

STATS INCREDIBLE!

56: Brian Roberts's total doubles in 2009, the single-season record for a switch hitter.

5: Postseason RBIs by Dave McNally in 1970. Ranks him tops (with Kerry Wood, 2003) among pitchers for a single postseason.

.332: Roberto Alomar's home field batting average at the O's Camden Yards, the highest mark in park history. Alomar also owns the top OBP (.400) and OPS (.907) there.

1.65: Zach Britton's ERA in 2014, making him the first pitcher in franchise history with a sub-2.00 ERA, SUB-1.000 WHIP, and 25+ saves. He repeated the feat in 2015.

31: Outfielder Brady Anderson's stolen base total in 1994. He finished ninth in baseball in stolen bases, and tied for 208th in caught stealing (1).

58: Home runs hit by the 1986 St. Louis Cardinals. The 1987 Orioles hit 58 home runs just in May.

53: Home runs hit by O's first baseman Chris Davis in 2013. The 1954 Orioles hit 52 home runs as a team.

61: Davis's home run total over a 162-game span, from August 18, 2012 to August 23, 2013.

11.5: Ripken's best single season WAR, in 1991. Babe Ruth had an 11.5 WAR in 1926, hitting .372 with 47 home runs and 153 RBIs.

.520: Outfielder Mark Deveraux's batting average with the bases loaded in 1992, collecting 38 RBIs.

10.69: ERA of O's starter Brian Matusz in 2011. It is the highest single-season ERA ever recorded (40 innings minimum).

BOSTON RED SOX

Est. 1901

Pedro Martinez had a 228 ERA+ from 1999 to 2003. His ERA+ over that five-year span tops the career-bests of Roger Clemens (226 ERA+, in 2005), Cy Young (219, 1901), Randy Johnson (197, 1997), Clayton Kershaw (197, 2014), and Nolan Ryan (195, 1981), to name a few.

The Boston Red Sox weren't always the "Red Sox," nor did they always wear red socks.

As part of the original eight franchises of the American League, Boston spent the first seven seasons of its existence with no official nickname. "Boston Americans" is sometimes credited as the first team moniker, although it was more of a clarification, as this club was the *American* league neighbor of the NL Boston Beaneaters (Braves).

When the Beaneaters ditched their red stockings and went with an all-white uniform in 1908, the no-name AL Boston squad seized the opportunity, adopted a new uniform, and officially became the Red Sox.

[FYI: The spelling of "Sox" was a somewhat popular abbreviation for "stockings" at the turn of the century. It was also a helpful shortcut for newspapers.]

The Sox are one of the most popular, storied franchises in baseball history. They were the first home of Babe Ruth—one of the most talented *pitchers* in the game (he threw 179.1 more innings than Hall of Famer Bruce Sutter)—and Ted Williams, the man in the conversation with Babe as perhaps the greatest hitter, ever.

More recently, the Sox have won 25% of the World Series between 2004 and 2015 (2004, 2007, 2013), but have, famously, not always had the ball bounce their way.

In 1918, Ruth was ninth in the league in ERA (2.22), and second in WHIP (1.046), while also leading all of baseball in home runs (11). He had 170 Ks in 1916 without giving up a single home run, which is still a franchise record.

Ace pitcher Babe Ruth, warming up for the Red Sox (between 1914–19). (Frances P. Burke)

In 1917, Ruth led the league in complete games, going 24–13 with a 2.01 ERA. Ty Cobb, during the only season in which he led the majors in at-bats (588), struck out 34 times; 11.8% of those came from pitches thrown by the Great Bambino.

This was the guy Boston traded to the rival Yankees for $100,000 in 1919. Boston had won three of the previous four World Series with Ruth on the roster, while the Yanks were still searching for their first World Series victories.

In 2004, when Boston lifted "The Curse of the Bambino" by finally winning another championship, New York had twenty-six under its belt.

Cy Young

Cy Young (SP, 1901–08), in his day, was perhaps the game's greatest pitcher. Since, he's been all but dehumanized, as the namesake of Major League Baseball's award for each league's top arm. The name "Cy Young" is alive and well, but is most routinely associated with the accomplishments of other players.

Lest we forget—

Young joined the upstart American League and Boston Americans in 1901 with a stellar reputation, racking up 286 wins in just 11 seasons in the National League. He led the league in victories his first three seasons with Boston, and averaged 24 wins, with a 2.00 ERA during his eight-year stint with the team. His ERA was over a full run higher in the NL (3.06).

He had four seasons with at least 20 wins, a sub-2.00 ERA, and a sub-1.000 WHIP, and only Walter Johnson had more (7). Remarkably, he seemed to get *much* better with age, pitching a career-best 1.26 ERA at the age of forty-one in 1908. If he stopped pitching at the age of forty-three in 1910, he would have had an ERA below 2.00 (1.95) through 1,100 innings in his 40s. Still, his 2.14 ERA as a quadragenarian is an MLB record (200 IP minimum), which he shares with

Eddie Plank. Consider—*when Young was born in 1867, life expectancy was around 40 years!*

The Cyclone had uncanny control of his craft, and remains the only pitcher in baseball history to throw consecutive seasons with 200+ strikeouts and 30 or fewer walks (1904–05). In fact, only Roy Halladay (2010) and Cliff Lee (2012) have done it in a single season since.

Ted Williams

Teddy Ballgame was a baseball savant. He hit 521 home runs, with a .344 career average, despite missing three full seasons to serve in World War II, and nearly two more to the Korean War. He famously batted .406 in 1941, won the Triple Crown in 1942 (.356, 36 HRs, 137 RBIs), served in the Marine Corps, was named MVP his very first season back in 1946, and then won another Triple Crown in 1947.

Teddy Ballgame being sworn in to the US Navy—May 22, 1942.
(PD-USGOV-MILITARY-MARINES)

[H-E-R-O: During the Korean War, Williams flew 39 combat missions. He was struck by enemy fire on three different occasions, and was awarded three air medals . . . and, yeah, he also played 43 games for the Sox, batting .406/.508/.901.]

Ruth once remarked to Williams that he hoped the Splendid Splinter would make a run at his career home run record. Hank Aaron eventually became the man to do it, and it's ironic that Williams (1939) and Aaron (1954) both share the anniversary of their first home run—April 23.

Aaron's 755 home runs may have dwarfed Wiliams' total, but if every one of Teddy's home runs (521), and doubles (525) were changed to strikeouts, his career on-base percentage (OBP) would still be 0.00087 higher than Aaron's.

His .450 career OBP against the Chicago White Sox was his worst against any other team, but is still higher than the OBP of baseball's current all-time home run champion, Barry Bonds (.444).

Also, Williams had five seasons in which he had at least 100 more walks than strikeouts. Bonds had two such seasons, while the Great Bambino had nary a single one.

There have only been 19 separate .500+ OBP seasons in baseball history, yet Williams *averaged* a .505 mark from 1941–49. Here is a breakdown of his OBP in select 162-game stretches:

First 162 games: .435

Worst 162 games: .404*

Best 162 games: .549

Last 162 games: .442

*Hall of Famers Cal Ripken Jr., Dave Winfield, Ernie Banks, Yogi Berra, and Jim Rice, between them, never once registered a single .404-or-higher OBP season.

In Williams's final season in 1960, he compiled an OPS+ of 190, at the age of forty-two. In 2013, thirty-year-old Miguel Cabrera had a career-high 190+ and won the AL MVP.

Williams batted an impressive .361 at Fenway Park, but he's not the park's all-time leader. That honor, at .369, belongs to . . .

Wade Boggs

Wade Boggs (3B, 1982–92) hit .338 in eleven seasons with Boston, winning five batting titles—four of which were consecutive, from 1985–88. But whether he got his bat on the ball or not, Boggs was simply one of the best ever at getting on base. Some facts and figures about Boggs that support this assertion:

- Led the American League for five straight seasons in on-base percentage, from 1985–89.
- Led all of baseball in times he reached base safely for *seven* straight seasons, from 1983–89.
- His .463 OBP from 1986–88 is the same as Joe DiMaggio's OBP during his famous 56-game hit streak in 1941.
- In games in which Boggs had at least one strikeout, his OBP was still .341. Cal Ripken Jr. had a .340 OBP for his entire career.
- Only player in history to have four straight seasons with at least 200 hits and 100 walks (1986–89).
- Had four seasons with at least 200 hits, including 50+ for extra bases, and 100+ walks. Babe Ruth had only three such seasons.
- Roger Maris had a 167 OPS+ the year he hit 61 home runs in 1961. In 1988, Boggs hit just five home runs and had a 168 OPS+.
- Had two seasons with at least 150 singles, 50 extra-base hits, and 100 walks. Every other player in history, combined? Zero.
- Boggs reached base safely in 152 games in 1985—most in a season in baseball history.

Perhaps the ultimate sign of respect for the scrappy hitter: Boggs led the league in intentional walks for six straight years, from 1987–92. He totaled just 53 home runs during that span.

New Millennium, New Results

The Sox have completely shed their reputation as the hardluck loser, which hung like a fog over the franchise after Ruth's departure.

Boston is the first and only team to successfully come back from an 0–3 deficit in a playoff series, discarding the rival Yankees in a dramatic 2004 ALCS. They rode the high to a quick victory over the St. Louis Cardinals in the World Series, and suddenly the hex was gone.

Curt Schilling *(P, 2004–07)* was a big part of the solution, going 21–6 with a 3.26 ERA in 2004 and finishing as runner-up for the AL Cy Young. He faced 910 batters that season and got ahead in the count 0–2 against 240 of them without surrendering a single walk. He averaged a 4.383 strikeout-to-walk ratio over his 20-year MLB career, second only to Tommy Bond (5.036 K/BB), who last pitched in 1884—during a time when as many as *nine* balls were required for a walk!

Schilling is probably best remembered as a *gamer*, as evidenced by his career +4.092 WPA (Win Probability Added) in the postseason, the highest ever for a starting pitcher. He was instrumental in two of Boston's championship runs (2004, 2007), compiling a 2–0 record, with a 0.79 ERA in World Series starts for the Sox.

One of his predecessors, **Pedro Martinez** *(P, 1998–04)*, was 16–9 with a 3.90 ERA in '04, but he was much, *much* better than that overall during his Red Sox career. In his five seasons prior, Martinez was a combined 82–21 with an ERA of just 2.10. He had four qualified seasons during that stretch with an ERA below 2.30, and had five such seasons total throughout his career. No other pitcher since 1915 has had more.

In 1999, he faced 314 batters with runners on base, and did not allow a single home run to any of them. The following season, Pedro tossed an AL-best 1.74 ERA that was a ridiculous 35.4% of the league average. *He would have still led the league in ERA if his ERA was doubled.*

Pedro was a first-ballot election to the Hall of Fame in 2015, and it was a no-brainer. The 1999 Triple Crown winner (23 Ws/ 2.07 ERA/ 313 Ks) had a 2.20 ERA through seven straight seasons, from 1997–2003. Hall of Famers Nolan Ryan, Bob Feller, Warren Spahn, Lefty Grove, and Phil Niekro all only had just one season in their careers with an ERA that low.

On the offensive side, **David Ortiz** *(DH, 2003–15)* has been a mainstay at first base/DH for the Sox since 2003. He earned All-Star and Silver Slugger honors for each of Boston's last three championship seasons (2004, 2007, 2013).

Big Papi, after a 37-homer campaign in 2015, has nine career 30-home run seasons (all with Boston), one more than Ted Williams (8). He is the all-time leader among DHs in home runs (447) and slugging percentage (.554). However, the 2013 World Series MVP seemed to make his greatest contributions on the game's biggest stage.

Ortiz compiled a career slash line of .455/.576/.795 in World Series play, the best batting average, on-base percentage, and slugging percentage ever among players with at least 35 plate appearances.

STATS INCREDIBLE!

.304: Outfielder Carl Yastrzemski's "diminutive" batting average over a six-year span in which he won three batting titles (1963–68).

12.4: Yastrzemski's WAR in 1967, making him the only player not named Babe Ruth with a single season position player WAR that high. He reached base 5,305 times in his career—more than the Babe, and fifth-most all-time.

.476: Boggs's on-base percentage in 1988, the highest OBP by a player with single-digit home runs since Tris Speaker's .483 (with 8 HR) in 1920.

80%: The percentage of games in which Boggs reached base—according to his Hall of Fame plaque. This is an error. He reached base safely in 85.2%.

12: The Red Sox selected Nomar Garciaparra 12th overall in 1994. He accumulated a 44.2 WAR for his career, while selections 1-11 combined for just a 35.2.

.406: Ted Williams's batting average in 1941, the last .400 batting average season in baseball. His 1.287 OPS that year was the highest in baseball history for a .400 season.

.1433: The differential of Williams's 1941 batting average to the league average. This was the largest batting average differential during the Live Ball Era.

9: Home runs allowed by Pedro Martinez through 213⅓ innings in 1999. Each one was just a solo shot.

1942: The year shortstop Johnny Pesky led the AL in hits, as a rookie. He served three years in the Navy from 1943–45, and came back to lead the AL in hits in both 1946 and 1947.

13: The amount of home runs hit by Babe Ruth in games he pitched from 1914–19. He surrendered just 9 home runs in those games.

.00087: If all of Ted Williams's 521 home runs and 525 doubles were outs, he'd still have a .00087 higher on-base percentage than Hank Aaron.

.323: Red Sox Dom DiMaggio's batting average at Fenway Park—higher than brother Joe DiMaggio's average at Yankee Stadium (.315).

50/50: Red Sox player Tris Speaker became the first player in baseball history with 50 doubles and 50 stolen bases in the same season in 1912. The only player to do it since was Craig Biggio in 1998.

NEW YORK YANKEES

Est. 1901

The Yankees were never sub-.500 during any span of 162 games played by Derek Jeter.

Like it or not, the Yankees are "America's Team" in Major League Baseball. With a record 18 division titles, 40 American League titles, and 27 World Series championships, it's hard to argue otherwise. But, it didn't always look like things were going to turn out so great for the Yanks.

The Yankees actually started as the Baltimore Orioles in 1901, but not the modern Orioles we know today. They were initially denied access to the Big Apple by the National League's New York Giants in 1901 and had to set up shop in Baltimore instead. Perhaps fortuitously for the franchise, things went very wrong, very quickly.

It was a horrifically mismanaged franchise its first two seasons, and was given up to league control after a 50–88 showing in 1902. Before the start of the 1903 season, the league was able to overrule the Giants' objection and get the franchise moved to Manhattan, with new owners, as the New York Highlanders. But, because the franchise essentially folded, and was then sold to a separate location and ownership group, it's unclear whether the *team* was sold, or just the team's designated spot in the American League. Currently, most baseball historians consider the two completely separate franchises, especially since only five players (13%) remained on the club after the move. Either way, it was a shaky start.

The Highlanders/Yankees were unspectacular their first 17 years, averaging a 72–76 per season record over the stretch, while never reaching the World Series. Then came Babe Ruth—it was really just that simple.

Ruth had been one of the game's best pitchers, and part-time hitters, while with the Red Sox before being sold to New York. The acquisition turned the fortunes of both franchises, "cursing" the Sox into an 86-year playoff drought, all the while handing the Yankees one of the most dominant figures in American sports history. Of course, Ruth had some help.

In 1920, with Ruth hitting more home runs by himself (54) than any other *team* in the American League, maybe he didn't need help. But, over a 12-year period (1921–32), the Yankees really were one of the most dominant, and balanced, teams in history, reaching seven World Series and winning four (1923, 1927, 1928, 1932). After all, one single player doesn't explain a near-century of consistent excellence.

The Yankees have always been masters of reloading. You know the names—after Ruth and Lou Gehrig came Joe DiMaggio, Whitey Ford, Mickey Mantle, Reggie Jackson, Don Mattingly, Derek Jeter, and Mariano Rivera. Just to name a few. There's a legend (or two ... or five) for every era of Yankees baseball, and each one adds to the lure. But it all started with The Babe.

The Team that Ruth Built

When the Boston Red Sox famously shipped George Herman "Babe" Ruth to New York for the paltry sum of $100,000, the Yankees weren't just getting one of the game's best hitters *and* pitchers. They were also reeling in one of their most formidable opponents.

The Great Bambino's slash line against the Yankees to that point was .337/.438/.663 in 194 plate appearances. For comparison's sake, if not for Jose Altuve's .341 batting average, each one of those numbers would have been tops in all of Major League Baseball in 2014.

In addition, as a pitcher, Ruth compiled a 17–5 record and 2.21 ERA in 23 career starts against the Yanks. Again, for comparison, AL Cy Young Award winner, Corey Kluber, was 18–9 with a 2.44 ERA in 2014.

Ruth only pitched in five regular season games after joining the Yankees, so it's easy to forget he was one of the game's best hurlers. He led the league in ERA with the Red Sox in 1916 (23–12, 1.75), and his career 2.28 ERA (min. 1,000 innings pitched) has been bested just once since 1927—by future Hall of Famer, and lifetime Yankee, Mariano Rivera (2.21). Of course, the Babe didn't accrue nicknames like the Sultan of Swat and the Colossus of Clout without doing some pretty incredible things with a baseball bat.

Ruth is famous for his 714 home runs, good for third all-time, and he's the career leader in slugging percentage (.690), OPS (1.164), and OPS+ (206). But did you know . . . ?

- Ruth is the single season WAR leader amongst all MLB players for ages 25, 26, 28, 29, 31, 32, and 35.
- He batted .401 through a 255-game stretch from April 24, 1923 to August 8, 1924.

Babe Ruth, in 1920, his first season with the Yankees.
(Paul Thompson, 1920)

- His single-season best was 60 home runs, but Babe hit 71 in 162 games from July 24, 1927 to July 30, 1928.
- Babe mashed a record 365 home runs with runners on base. That is nine more than Hank Aaron, and 53 more than Barry Bonds.
- Qualified seasons with a slash line of at least .350/.500/.725: Babe Ruth, 5.
  Everyone else combined, 4.
- For nine separate seasons, Ruth managed a slugging percentage of at least .700. That is more than Barry Bonds, Ted Williams, Stan Musial, Mickey Mantle, and Sammy Sosa combined.
- If Ruth did the truly impossible and resurrected, returned to baseball, and struck out in 3,187 straight plate appearances, he would still have a slugging percentage of .500. This is the same mark as—and actually percentage points ahead of— Hall of Famer Ernie Banks. Additionally, Babe Ruth would have to resurrect, return to baseball, and go 0-for-1,147 for his slugging percentage to drop below Barry Bonds's .6069.
- Ruth averaged 10.56 WAR per 162-games played—the highest in baseball history. Mike Trout, one of today's biggest stars, ranks second with just over one less win. Remarkably, this does NOT factor in Ruth's 20.6 WAR as a pitcher.
- He would have to resurrect, return to baseball, and go 0-for-1,501—or 0-for-two full seasons—for his career OPS to dip below 1.000.
- He had 10 career steals of home. That is more than Rickey Henderson, Lou Brock, and Tim Raines had combined (9).
- He had three qualified seasons in which he batted at least .375/.500/.750. No other player in baseball history has even one.
- His 183.6 combined pitcher and position player WAR is 1.3 more than Derek Jeter and Tom Seaver had combined.
- Of his 714 career home runs, 84.5% (603) were record-breaking.

Babe Ruth, laying unconscious after colliding headfirst with the Washington Senators' outfield wall, at full-speed. Ruth finished the game 3-3, with two RBIs, and then played the second game of the double-header. He homered the following day. (LOC, nocc.11744)

56 in '41

Joltin' Joe DiMaggio picked up where Ruth left off, joining the Yankees in 1935, and matching the Babe's four World Series wins . . . in just four years. He had a .341/.391/.622 slash line during that period to start his career, in addition to winning the four straight rings. Historically, that was his *second*-most famous streak.

DiMaggio's 56-game hit streak is one of the most storied accomplishments in sports history, and when it ended July 17, 1941, the Yankee Clipper began a 16-game hit streak the very next day. In those 73 games, he batted .408.

Joe DiMaggio, in an offseason photo-op, kissing the bat that got him hits in 56 straight games in 1941. (The Sporting News Pub. Co., LOC)

Willie Keeler's 45-game hit streak in 1896–97 sits well behind in second place, but interestingly, Joe's brother Dom holds the 16th-best streak at 34 games in 1949. Even older brother Vince managed a 12-game streak in 1941 for Pittsburgh, the same season as Joe's.

In all but two seasons that DiMaggio and Boston rival Ted Williams played together from 1939 to 1951, there was not a single MVP election that did not feature one of the two, or both, in the top three in balloting, and they'd split five MVPs between them. In many ways, the argument still exists over who was better, but for the record, while DiMaggio racked up a .463 on-base percentage during his hit streak, Ted Williams put up a .482 OBP for his entire career.

[Just for fun— Pitchers Ted Lyons and Lefty Grove both surrendered a home run to Babe Ruth during his 60-home run season and a hit to Joltin' Joe during his tremendous streak.]

Next Verse, Same as the First

The Yankees are unlike any other franchise in sports because of their dominantly successful history. For seemingly every generation, they played best and had the best players. The Yanks appeared in 22 World Series during a 29-year period, from 1936 to 1964. But, considering the tremendous parity and continuous turnover that exists in the game today, it's *almost* as impressive that they haven't finished under .500 in any of the previous 23 seasons. Derek Jeter, Mariano Rivera, and a host of other recent Yankee greats have helped keep the legacy going.

Jeter, easily the Yankees' best shortstop, and in the argument for best player not named "Babe" in franchise history, leads the team all-time in hits (3,465), at-bats (11,195), doubles (544), and stolen bases (358).

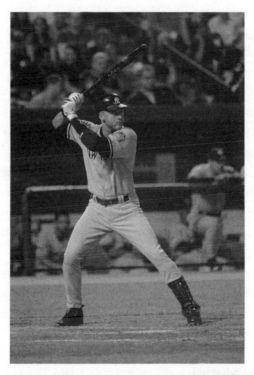

Yankee captain Derek Jeter's iconic batting stance, 2008. (Keith Allison, KeithAllisonPhoto.com)

In 2005, he clubbed a major-league record 66 opposite field hits. The next season, he hit 64—the second-most in recorded history.

Hall of Fame shortstop Ozzie Smith would have to return to baseball and hit 294 consecutive home runs to edge past Jeter in slugging percentage. Of course, Smith had 485 more defensive runs saved over the course of his career (+238.7 to -246.3), but I think Greg Maddux and Tom Glavine put it best:

"Chicks dig the long ball."

On the pitching side, it's hard to quantify the impact that MLB saves leader, Mariano Rivera, had on nearly two full decades of Yankees baseball—but we will try.

Rivera, who owned 20.4% of all saves in Yankees history at the time of his retirement in 2014 (652 of 3,190), had 366 more saves than walks surrendered in his career. Only seven players in history have more than 366 saves alone.

His career adjusted ERA+ (1,000 IP minimum) is staggeringly ahead of every other pitcher in baseball history. Rivera (205), is well ahead of runner-up Pedro Martinez (154), and even Cy Young himself (138). But it's what he did in the postseason that might make him the best Yankees hurler of all time.

In 141 career postseason innings, Rivera racked up an ERA of just 0.70, which ranks tops in history (25 IP minimum). He faced 527 postseason batters and only surrendered two home runs. The amount of runners (earned) who have scored on Rivera in the postseason (11) wouldn't even fill a jury pool.

Masahiro Tanaka, a current starting pitcher for New York, has done a great job thus far carrying the torch. The Japanese native had a decent 2015 (12–7, 3.51 ERA), but was remarkably dominant in his 2014 rookie season, which was Rivera's last in the big leagues.

Tanaka's 6.71 K/BB (100 IP minimum) was the best rookie mark since 1984, when Roger Clemens had a 4.34 K/BB as a rookie.

Tanaka was an All-Star in his record-breaking first season (13–5, 2.77), and has a bright future leading the new Yankees generation to future greatness.

STATS INCREDIBLE!

34.8%: The percentage of all World Series games through 2015 (225 of 646) in which the Yankees have been participants.

4: The number of seasons Lou Gehrig had at least 15 triples, 15 homers, and 100 walks. Every other player in history who achieved this mark did so twice. Both were Yankees—Babe Ruth in 1921 and Charlie Keller in 1940.

55: Times Yankees shortstop Frank Crosetti was hit by a pitch from 1932–38, most in the American League. With just under half as many during the same period, Lou Gehrig (27 HBP) was second in the AL. A study on the effects of concussions in 2010 left open the possibility that Lou Gehrig may not have actually had "Lou Gehrig's Disease" (ALS) when he died in 1941. Instead, frequent bean balls to the head (pre-helmet era) may have mimicked ALS symptoms.

14.7%: Percentage of Lou Gehrig's 102 career stolen bases that were steals of home (15).

.350/.470/.640: In a season with at least 700 plate appearances, only Lou Gehrig has slashed this high. And he did it four times.

.314: Joe DiMaggio never had a career batting average below .314 at the end of any given day throughout his Hall of Fame career.

206/122: For his career, Babe Ruth had a 206 OPS+ hitting, and 122 ERA+ pitching. Context: Mickey Mantle had a 206 OPS+ in 1961 with a career-high 54 home runs, and Nolan Ryan had a 123 ERA+ in 1973 when he set the modern-day strikeout record.

379: The amount of times Ruth reached base safely in 1923, most ever. In 1957, Mantle reached base safely 319 times, most ever for a switch-hitter.

114: The amount of home runs hit by Yankees teammates Mantle (54) and Roger Maris (61) combined in 1961. The Red Sox, as a team, hit 112 that year.

40: RBIs by Mickey Mantle in World Series play, an all-time record.

21: Mickey Mantle's career-high in stolen bases in 1959. This was the most ever by a player under Casey Stengel (managed 25 seasons).

90/40: In 2002, Alfonso Soriano became baseball's only player with at least 90 extra-base hits and 40 stolen bases in a single season.

5: Amount of qualified seasons in which a catcher had more home runs than strikeouts since 1940. They all belong to Yogi Berra.

TAMPA BAY RAYS

Est. 1998

On August 7, 1999, Wade Boggs became the 23rd member of the 3,000 hit club and the first ever to homer for hit number 3,000. Perhaps even more amazing is the fact that Tony Gwynn became the 22nd member just one day earlier.

While the Rays, formerly the Devil Rays until the 2008 season, have a dogged reputation for terrible attendance figures—the team has only twice finished in the top ten in AL attendance—its performance, overall, has been impressive. The Rays averaged 92 wins between 2008 and 2013. In 47 seasons, the Kansas City Royals have only managed five *total* seasons of 92 wins or more.

What the team needs most is time. Wade Boggs was the initial face of the franchise and finished his career with Tampa Bay, but the Rays currently have no team-associated Hall of Famers, and no significant historical tradition on which to fall back. Contrary to the mystical whispers in *Field of Dreams*, just building a major-league franchise is not enough. But winning is attractive and impossible to ignore. If they keep playing well, people will most definitely come.

The Devil's Rays

What's in a name? Tampa Bay secured its first winning season in franchise history and reached the World Series during its first season as the sun-centric "Rays." Until then, the "Devil Rays" were actually quite putrid. Then-owner Vince Naimoli picked the original name from over 7,000 fan suggestions in 1995, but managed just a .399 win percentage before the team's deviled logo turned sunny side up.

[Fun Fact: The now-defunct Maui Stingrays, of the Hawaiian Winter League, held a copyright which prevented Tampa from using the same name. At the time, religious fanatics had protested the use of the word "devil" in the team's alternative, so it was seemingly a doomed, and perhaps cursed, idea from the start.]

Swan Songs

In the early years of the franchise, Tampa Bay was a popular stop for big-name players whose careers were coming to an end.

Wade Boggs was one of the first, joining the team at its inception in 1998. He is still the only Hall of Famer to don the uniform, and a very lonely list of team HOFers on the Rays' website backs this up. But Boggs's final 727 farewell at-bats in Tampa were anything but sad.

He's currently ranked seventh in franchise history in batting average (minimum 700 at-bats), and pulled off a slash line of .333/.430/.442 in his final 50 games.

"Crime Dog" Fred McGriff was another MLB great that finished his career in Tampa, but those final 72 at-bats in 2004 do not adequately tell the story of his Rays career. He batted just .181 that year, and finished seven jacks short of the 500-homer club. It was a poor finale, but McGriff was brilliant in the franchise's first 3+ seasons (1998–2001).

Coming in, Boggs was the future Hall of Famer, but McGriff was that team's most productive player. He earned All-Star honors in 2000, mashed 99 home runs (seventh all-time in franchise history), and at .864, still has the team's highest career OPS (minimum 2,000 at-bats). Of course, if one were to drop the at-bat minimum to 600, the franchise leader would be Jose Canseco (.898 OPS, 648 AB)—and it starts to become clear that Tampa may not have had a flawless organizational plan from the start.

Canseco's 34 homers in 1999 are still the most in team history for a right-handed hitter, but he epitomized what was wrong with the Rays' plan. In 2000, the meat of the Rays batting order was McGriff, Canseco, and newcomers Greg Vaughn and Vinny Castilla. They are all members of the 300 career home run club, sure, but they were also decidedly old (average 34.25 years) and slow (13 collective stolen bases) compared to the average ballplayer at that time. Tampa's power push led to a mere 69 wins in 2000 and did nothing to push the franchise forward.

On a Brighter Note

We did mention the Rays have done some good things too, right?

It hasn't yet logged 20 years in Major League Baseball, but the team still owns the single-season postseason record for stolen bases—24 in 2008.

James Shields is the only Ray to win a World Series game, and David Price is the team's lone Cy Young winner. The last, and only, Rays pitcher to toss two consecutive shutouts? Rolando Arrojo aligned those stars back in 1998. But, the new kid on the block, 2015 All-Star Chris Archer, is the only Tampa hurler to make four consecutive starts without surrendering an earned run.

Really, an increased focus on young, talented pitching is what has turned around the team's fortunes. In 2014, Rays pitchers struck out 1,437 batters, second-most all-time, trailing only the Indians' 1,450—also in 2014.

In Archer (2015: 12–13, 3.23 ERA) and Alex Cobb (2014: 10–9, 2.87 ERA), the Rays have a talented, young pitching duo to build around. They are the only two pitchers in franchise history with ERAs below 3.35 after their first four MLB seasons. Cobb is currently coming back from Tommy John surgery, but the Rays have had capable arms holding down the fort. Of the seven under-27 AL pitchers with a sub-4.00 ERA last year, three were Rays: Archer, Jake Odorizzi (25; 9–9, 3.35 ERA), and Erasmo Ramirez (25; 11–6, 3.75 ERA).

Admittedly, not all the "good" stats harbor a promising future, and such is the case for Nick Franklin in 2013, who was the fastest rookie second baseman to hit 10 home runs (52 games) since Joe Gordon in 1938. However, Franklin hit just two more in his remaining 50 games that season, and currently plays for the AAA Durham Bulls.

Evan Longoria, the Rays' career WAR leader (42.6).
(Keith Allison, KeithAllisonPhoto.com)

Still, the Rays finished with a better record last season (2015: 80–82; 2014: 77–85), despite losing two of their best pitchers in 2014 (Price and Cobb). Tampa Bay no longer has the reputation of the reliable doormat, which comes with being an expansion franchise. The Mets turned things around quickly with dominant pitching in 2015, and the Rays are probably a good candidate to follow that mold, as early as 2016.

STATS INCREDIBLE!

271: Strikeouts for David Price in 2014, with the Rays and Tigers. Most by a traded pitcher since Randy Johnson had 329 Ks in 1998.

1,221⅓: Babe Ruth's career innings pitched, with a sparkling 122 ERA+. Through David Price's first 1,221⅓ innings, he compiled a nearly-identical 121 ERA+.

104: Strikeouts for relief pitcher Brad Boxberger in 2014, who became the first Tampa Bay pitcher in history with at least 100 Ks without making a single start.

30/10: Ben Zobrist is the first and only player in team history with 30+ doubles and 10+ homers in four consecutive seasons (2011–14).

20: Evan Longoria is the first player in Rays history with seven straight 20+ home run seasons. No other player even has five such seasons.

31: Jose Canseco's home run total through 81 games in 1999, before his season was derailed due to injuries.

15/15/50: In 2006, outfielder Carl Crawford became the only American Leaguer *ever* with a 15+ triple/ 15+ home run/ 50+ stolen base season.

TORONTO BLUE JAYS

Est. 1977

In 2000, Carlos Delgado had a 1.134 OPS—the highest ever single-season mark by a player to appear in at least 162 games. His 181 OPS+ is also tops.

The Blue Jays are the only Canadian team in Major League Baseball, and are still relatively new in the scope of the game's storied history overall. However, baseball has deep roots in Canada that extend as far back as the game itself.

There is evidence to suggest that the very first recorded game took place in Ontario in 1838, albeit a very crude version that included five bases and an undefined fair/foul territory. Canada also lays claim to the first home run of Babe Ruth's professional career.

On September 5, 1914, Ruth, playing for the minor league Providence Grays, hit his first homer at Hanlan's Point Stadium in Toronto, a 3-run shot to go with his complete game, one-hit shutout of the Maple Leafs.

Canada was actually a hotbed for minor league teams for much of the twentieth century, and while Toronto had to wait until 1977 to land a major-league squad of its own, it wasted little time building a contender. Sure, the team finished dead last in five of its first six seasons, but by 1983, the Jays started an 11-year run in which the team would never finish less than 5 games above .500.

Toronto won its first World Series in 1992 with a good mix of young stars (Roberto Alomar, John Olerud), and ageless vets (Dave Winfield, Jack Morris). Joe Carter then capped the Blue Jays' successful run with a walk-off World Series–winning homer in 1993 to repeat as champs, and, really . . . that has been about it.

The Blue Jays, just recently in 2015, had their first 90-win season and first playoff berth since Carter's magic shot over 22 years ago. But, for fans of teams like the title-less Astros, surely a decade-long run and a couple of trophies would be nothing to scoff at.

The Championship Run

Pat Gillick, the Hall of Fame GM for the Blue Jays at the time, gets a lot of credit for building a contender in Toronto, and for good reason. Both of the Jays' championship squads featured predominantly traded-for players or free agent signees (aside from John Olerud). Gillick was an ace at picking from other teams' talent.

The list of key contributors from those squads is certainly a roll call of some of the game's best, though they're not always players most fondly remembered as Blue Jays.

John Olerud *(TOR 1989–96):* Selected in the third round of the 1989 draft by Toronto, Olerud was a pillar of the team's offense for several years. He was a major contributor during the team's 1992 WS run, but wouldn't become its brightest star until the following season.

That year, Olerud batted a league-high .363, setting the Blue Jays franchise mark for single season batting average, while compiling the eleventh-best OPS+ (186) in the American League since 1980. The great Willie Mays never had a single-season OPS+ that high, mustering "just" a 185 in 1965.

Olerud also flirted with .400 late into the season, eclipsing the mark as late as August 2, but finished the year out batting just .290 the rest of the way.

He's one of the greatest Blue Jays of all time, and despite boasting a better OBP than 79.9% of all position players enshrined in Baseball's Hall of Fame, Olerud garnered just four votes in his first, and last, year on the HOF ballot.

Roberto Alomar *(1991–95):* Toronto pulled off a wonderful trade in 1990, landing future Hall of Famer Alomar and Joe Carter from the Padres for Fred McGriff and Tony Fernandez.

Alomar was an All-Star and Gold Glover each of his five seasons in Toronto, and holds the second-highest career batting average in team history (.307), second only to Paul Molitor (.315).

In 1993, Alomar became just the fourth player in MLB history with a .400+ OBP, 55+ stolen bases, and more home runs than times caught stealing. Simply put—Alomar was an all-around threat and incredibly efficient.

Jimmy Key *(1984–92):* Key was only 13–13 his final season in Toronto, but he pitched to a 1.50 ERA in postseason play, earning two wins, including a relief W in the deciding Game 6 of the '92 World Series.

Key was a finesse pitcher with tremendous control. He led the league with just 1.1 BB/9 in 1989. In 1990, he threw a first-pitch strike to 254 batters and did not issue a walk to a single one of them.

Jack Morris *(1992–93)* and **Dave Winfield** *(1992):* Morris was a key free agent acquisition for the Jays prior to the 1992 season, leading the team as well as the league with 21 wins despite, at age thirty-seven, being the second-oldest player on the team. The oldest? Winfield (forty), who was just the sixth player with a 26-home run season after age thirty-nine.

Individual Champs

Since 1993, the Jays haven't won much team hardware, but they haven't been short on individual accomplishments.

Roger Clemens, winning consecutive Cy Youngs for Toronto in 1997 (21–7, 2.05 ERA, 292 Ks) and 1998 (20–6, 2.65 ERA, 271 Ks), became just the fourth hurler in MLB history to achieve pitching's Triple Crown (league leader in wins, ERA, and strikeouts) in two straight seasons. He was the first and last AL pitcher to do it in consecutive seasons since Lefty Grove in 1930–31.

Roy Halladay was the last Cy Young winner for the Blue Jays (2003), and accumulated the second-most wins in team history (148; Dave Stieb, 175). He is the last pitcher to toss consecutive shutouts for Toronto (September 25 and 30, 2009) and is the only pitcher in MLB history to have five seasons of 200+ strikeouts along with 40 or fewer walks. No other player even had four such seasons.

The individual stars seemed to have converged recently with Toronto, as sluggers Jose Bautista (40 HRs), Edwin Encarnacion (39 HRs), and Josh Donaldson (41 HRs) combined for 120 home runs in 2015—as many as all 51 players to swing a bat with the Marlins last season.

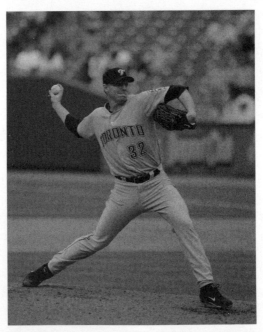

It never translated to postseason berths, but, at times, the Jays had the best pitcher in baseball in Roy Halladay. (Keith Allison, KeithAllisonPhoto.com)

Bautista hit almost as many home runs his first full season in Toronto (54; 2010) as he did his first six seasons in the big leagues combined (59; 2004–09). In 2015, he had his fourth 35+ homer/100+ walk season, the most of any active player.

Encarnacion has averaged 38 homers his past four years, and Donaldson, in 2015, became just the seventh third baseman in league history with a 40+ homer season. Josh Donaldson was a pleasant surprise for the Jays in 2015, to put it mildly. The fifth-year third baseman arrived in Toronto via trade from Oakland and promptly slashed .297/.371/.568, with 41 homers during his first season in blue. Donaldson led the league in runs scored (122), RBIs (123), and total bases (352), and became the Blue Jays' first AL MVP recipient since George Bell in 1987. With 41 doubles on the season, Donaldson became just the third player in team history with a 40 2B/40 HR season, and the first since Carlos Delgado in 2000 (Shawn Green, 1999).

His combined WAR for 2014–15 (16.1) was just a shade below Mike Trout's (17.3), and it's a testament to Donaldson's well-balanced game, at the plate and in the field. In 2015, he became the first third baseman with at least 40 home runs, 70 walks, and 10 defensive runs saved since Mike Schmidt in 1980.

STATS INCREDIBLE!

43.77%: The 2010 Toronto squad is the only team in MLB history to have over 40% of its hits go for extra bases.

18.84%: The Jays had 1,364 hits, of which 257 were home runs, in 2010. It is the best home run percentage in MLB history.

.470: Carlos Delgado's OBP in 2000. It's the highest ever single-season mark for a player who appeared in at least 162 games.

4: Home runs hit by Carlos Delgado in a single game on September 25, 2003. He's the only player in history to hit four home runs in a game in which he had just four plate appearances.

3: The amount of players on the 1991 Blue Jays with 40+ doubles and 20+ stolen bases (Roberto Alomar, Devon White, Joe Carter). Only seven other teams in baseball history even had two such players.

50/25: The 2001 Blue Jays were the only team in baseball history to have all three of their outfielders reach 50 extra-base hits and 25 stolen bases.

42: Jose Bautista pulled 42 consecutive home runs to left field, from September 28, 2009 to August 16, 2010.

55/20: The '85 Jays team is the first in history to get 55+ extra-base hits and 20+ stolen bases from each of its three starting outfielders (Jesse Barfield, George Bell, Lloyd Moseby). The only other team to accomplish the feat was the 2001 Jays (Jose Cruz, Raul Mondesi, Shannon Stewart).

10.64: ERA of two-time Cy Young winner Roy Halladay in 2000, his third year with Toronto. From 1871 to today, it is the highest single-season ERA of any pitcher with at least 50 innings pitched.

3: Halladay had three seasons in which he averaged 6.25+ strikeouts-per-walk over at least 220 innings. This is the most since Tommy Bond had his fourth . . . in 1884, when six balls were required for free pass.

AMERICAN LEAGUE CENTRAL

CHICAGO WHITE SOX

Est. 1901

From July 27, 1954 to June 25, 1959, Nellie Fox played 741 games. He was hit-by-pitch more times (60) than he struck out (59).

The Chicago White Sox were one of the eight charter franchises of the upstart 1901 American League, and were a powerhouse from the onset, with an average record of 82–66 (.554) their first ten seasons of play.

Chicago won the league title that first year, but the World Series wasn't a thing until 1903. They won one of those in 1906, and another in 1917, but would reach just three World Series over the next 99 years (L, 1919; L, 1959; W, 2005). Why the sudden, dramatic drop off? A conspiracy, maybe?

Several key members of the 1919 squad took bribes and conspired to throw the World Series during a 5–3 series loss to the Cincinnati Reds in a rare best-of-nine-games format. Commissioner Kenesaw "Mountain" Landis ordered lifetime bans for eight of the reported conspirators, including Ed Cicotte and "Shoeless" Joe Jackson, two would-be Hall of Famers who remain banned to this day. With the team gutted of eight of its best players following the 1920 season, the "Black Sox" began a long journey back to glory.

In 2005, staff ace Mark Buehrle, and slugger Paul Konerko led the team to its first World Championship in 88 years—which is a mighty leap. Things like frozen food, microwaves, and television were all invented between White Sox championships—which made eating a TV dinner and watching them win a title on the tube a surely new and exhilarating proposition in 2005. But the in-between Shoeless Joe–to–Konerko era also had its fair share of exciting moments and players.

Just to name a few: Hall of Famers Ted Lyons, Luke Appling, Nellie Fox, Goose Gossage, Carlton Fisk, and Frank Thomas all made baseball interesting between championships on the South Side of Chicago. From 1951 to 1967, the club had a franchise record string of 17 straight winning seasons, mostly under the ownership of the enigmatic and inventive Bill Veeck (see Baltimore Orioles). They reached the ALCS in 1983 and 1993 before Wild Card playoff expansion, and won the AL Central in 2000.

Things could have been different, and the White Sox might have given the Yankees some good competition over the years, if not for the Black Sox scandal. Still, it's hard to ignore the great— though abridged—careers of the players responsible.

The Black Sox
The moniker given to the 1919 club plays like the stain of an old, ugly tattoo on the franchise. The players were great, and just as the movie *Eight Men Out* advertises quite literally in the title, only eight of them were responsible. Whether guilty or innocent of throwing ballgames, some incredibly talented ballplayers wore the uniform.

A 1920 newspaper collage after the Black Sox scandal broke.
(Underwood & Underwood, via *The Sporting News*, October 7, 1920)

Banned: Joe Jackson, an outfielder who earned the nickname "Shoeless" after hitting a triple while barefoot in the minor leagues, was arguably the most talented of the lot. His career batting average (.356) ranks third all-time, and his .383 average in 1920 is the highest ever for a player in his final season. His application for reinstatement was most recently denied in 2015, despite convincing evidence that he did nothing to throw the Series.

Cleared: Eddie Collins didn't take part in the fix, and, in an ironic juxtaposition to Jackson (whose brilliant career was cut short), played 25 MLB seasons, which ties him with Rickey Henderson for the most by any single position player.

His 3,315 hits are tops among second basemen, and good for 11th overall on baseball's all-time list. He rarely missed the ball, striking out just 205 times in his White Sox career (1915–26). By comparison, ChiSox DH Adam Dunn struck out 222 times in a single season in 2012.

Banned: The Black Sox ace, Ed Cicotte, sits fourth in team history in ERA (2.25) and eighth in wins (156). He pitched three sub-2.00 ERA seasons his last five years in the bigs before his lifetime ban. He is one of just eight players in history with five qualified sub-2.00 ERA seasons, tied with Ed Walsh, his rotation mate for five years, who finished his career with an MLB record 1.82.

Best Bats

The White Sox have reached the World Series just twice since 1919, but they have fielded some of the best players in baseball over the years.

Luke Appling, who is generally considered among the top five shortstops in the game's history, played 20 years in his MLB career, all for the White Sox. He is the franchise leader in career WAR (74.5), and holds the club record in single season batting average (.388, 1936). His .399 on-base percentage, is second among shortstops only to the .406 posted by Arky Vaughan, whose 14 years in baseball were played opposite Appling in the National League.

Appling played consistently well into his forties, playing three full seasons as a quadragenarian before retiring at age forty-four. He is the only shortstop in baseball's modern era, over any measurable span of at-bats, to maintain a .300 average after age forty (.301, 1,620 at-bats).

Nellie Fox, a scrappy, Hall of Fame second baseman, played 14 seasons with Chicago (1950–63) and was, stylistically, an Eddie Collins clone.

Like Collins, Fox, nicknamed Mighty Mite, didn't have much power (35 career home runs), but he was relentless in the batter's box, and one of the toughest hitters in the history of the game to strike out. In each of his 19 seasons, five of which he led the league in plate appearances, he never struck out more than 18 times. Fox had 15 qualified seasons with less than 20 strikeouts, which is the most in the modern era. Only 26 times (among 17 players) since Fox's retirement in 1965 has a player finished a qualified season with less than 20 strikeouts.

Frank Thomas (six-foot-five, 240 lbs), the Big Hurt, was a mountain in the batter's box. When he joined the team in 1990, Thomas was the tallest batter in team history, and the heaviest, taking the Burger King crown from Bob "Fatty" Fothergill (five-foot-ten, 235 lbs), a corner outfielder for the ChiSox in the 1930s. Like a Fatty Fothergill silhouette, the Big Hurt's game was well-rounded.

Thomas, a first baseman, has five seasons that rank in the franchise's top 10 in offensive WAR (1991–94, 1997), and is the White Sox career leader in total oWAR (74.4). He also holds career franchise records in on-base percentage (.427), slugging (.568), runs scored (1,327), doubles (447), home runs (448), and RBIs (1,465)—just to name a few.

He has the highest on-base percentage (.419) of any right-handed batter since 1946. He reached base in 87.9% of his 2,322 career games, and, in the AL, only Babe Ruth (.467) and Ted Williams (.488) reached base at a higher frequency through their first eight seasons than Thomas (.452).

Arms Race

The argument over who could be considered the best pitcher in team history is a good one, because a number of players make a very solid claim to the title. Not a single player appears twice in the top spot for the franchise lead in WAR (among pitchers; Red Faber, 68.4), ERA (Ed Walsh, 1.81), wins (Ted Lyons, 260), WHIP (Hoyt Wilhelm, 0.935), and strikeouts (Billy Pierce, 1796).

The cases for Faber and Lyons, White Sox teammates from 1923–33, are based on the same factor—longevity. Lyons played 21 years in the big leagues, all with Chicago, while Faber lasted 20, also all with Chicago. While Lyons leads the franchise in wins, he also leads in losses (230), and Faber is second in both categories (254–213).

Lyons was perhaps more consistent along the way, as Faber averaged just an annual 9–10 record with a 3.85 ERA during his final 10 seasons in the big leagues.

Walsh may lead the team, and all of baseball, in career ERA, but he only pitched seven full seasons in the majors—the same amount of seasons Wilhelm pitched dominantly in relief in a White Sox uniform.

Only one-third of Old Sarge's 21-year career was spent in Chicago, but he averaged a 1.92 ERA in that span, second in team history. And although he was not a starter, he was much more than a specialist, averaging 113 innings per season. No other pitcher since 1916 has had more relief appearances of 3+ innings than Wilhelm (197).

Of course, Mark Buerhle, who doesn't lead the franchise in any meaningful pitching category, was the team's best pitcher on their only World Series winner of the Live Ball Era.

He was a marvel of consistency, averaging 14 victories with a 3.81 ERA in his 11 full seasons with Chicago. His 14 seasons of at least 200 innings pitched are the 13th-most in MLB history—and he pitched them all consecutively, from 2001–14. Buehrle came up just 1.1 innings shy of 200 in 2015, which would have given Buerhle 14 American League 200+ IP seasons, good for second place behind the great Walter Johnson (18).

Chris Sale has a long way to go, but the current White Sox ace, an All-Star each of the past four seasons, is already breaking records. His K/BB rate each year from 2013–15 (4.91, 5.33, 6.52 respectively) are the top three in franchise history. Each of the past four seasons, Sale has set a new ChiSox record for strikeout percentage (24.9%, 26.1%, 30.4%, 33.29%, respectively).

STATS INCREDIBLE!

.424: Frank Thomas's on-base percentage with two strikes in 1994.

54: Outfielder Minnie Miñoso's age during two games in which he appeared for the White Sox, becoming the second-oldest position player in modern baseball history, and joining Nick Altrock as the only players in MLB history to play in five decades.

5: The number of White Sox players to hit at least 25 home runs in 2012, none of whom had 100 RBIs. The 2012 Sox is the only team in history with five 25+ homer, sub-100 RBI batters.

35: In 2014, outfielder José Abreu joined Albert Pujols (2001) and Hal Trosky (1934) as the only players to hit 35+ doubles and 35+ home runs during their rookie season.

200/1.000: In 2014, Chris Sale became the first White Sox pitcher since Ed Walsh in 1910 with 200+ strikeouts and a sub-1.000 WHIP.

CLEVELAND INDIANS

Est. 1901

In 1948, Lou Boudreau won the American League MVP Award. He had 10.4 WAR to just nine strikeouts. He was both the starting shortstop and the manager of the 1948 World Champion Indians.

The Cleveland Indians were one of the original eight charter franchises of the American League in 1901. They started out as the "Bluebirds" and wouldn't become the iconic "Indians" we know today until 1915. But, for a 12-year run in between, Cleveland's major-league ball club would actually be named after its team captain.

Star second baseman Napolean "Nap" Lajoie had just batted .426 for the AL's Philadelphia Athletics in 1901—a modern era MLB record that still stands—but the young phenom was not long for Philly. Due to being "poached" from the Athletics' National League counterpart, the Philadelphia Phillies, Lajoie was suddenly the primary object of desire in a brutal city turf war. The courts eventually ruled that the Phillies were the only team in Philadelphia that Lajoie could legally join for the 1902 season, and so A's owner Connie Mack threw *brotherly love* out the window and sold his rights to Cleveland. By 1903, the Cleveland Naps were born.

Lajoie was an instant hit in his new digs, leading the AL with a .378 average, and helping improve the club's record by 15 games from the previous season. A newspaper write-in contest locked in "Naps" as the new nickname in 1903, and Lajoie certainly did his best to earn the title.

In his 13-year stint with Cleveland, Lajoie batted .339 (third-best in franchise history) and even had a five-year turn as player-manager. The Naps' average record from 1903 until Lajoie's departure following the 1914 season was just 78–79, but it was enough to build upon toward a prosperous future.

Local baseball writers decided on "Indians" for the club starting in 1915, and the franchise's first championship in 1920 (5–2 over the Brooklyn Robins/Dodgers) helped make the moniker stick.

World Series appearances have been historically scarce for the ball club, as Cleveland has made it there just five times, winning once (1948), since Hall of Famer Tris Speaker helped get the Indians over the hump in 1920.

Napolean Lajoie, leading the team that bore his name, the Naps of 1903. (Chicago Daily News, LOC)

Regardless, just as Lajoie was the spark to keep the Cleveland franchise chugging along at the dawn of the twentieth century, the Indians have always had Hall of Famers in the mix to keep things interesting.

Nap vs. Shoeless Joe

Despite what the team's nickname might intimate, the Naps era of Cleveland baseball was not a one-man show. Nap Lajoie was the leader, but "Shoeless" Joe Jackson was, at least for a time, the team's best player.

Jackson racked up a .375 batting average during his six seasons with Cleveland, and .381 with a 1.000 OPS during the five years he played with Lajoie. His .408 average in 1911 and .395 in 1912 are the top two marks in team history.

He accumulated more triples (26) than strikeouts (19) in 1912, becoming one of just seven men in the modern era to hit 20 or more triples with less than 20 strikeouts in a single season. And Jackson is the only one to accomplish this twice (1920, CHW; 20 3B, 14 Ks).

With some of the greatest legends in baseball history in Walter Johnson, Ty Cobb, Tris Speaker, and Eddie Collins dominating the league, the Naps needed Jackson and Lajoie at their best, but Jackson missed significant time in 1910 and Lajoie missed 107 games between 1911–12. Unfortunately for Cleveland, Lajoie's prime never really matched up with Jackson's.

His first three seasons with the team, Lajoie batted .366, winning two batting titles. His play was a bit spotty after that, perhaps due to added responsibilities that came with taking on the skipper role (1905–09) and various odd injuries—including blood poisoning from the dye in his red socks in 1905. Still, he won his fifth batting title in 1910 (.384), and was surely one of the game's all-time best.

Among second basemen in MLB history, only Rogers Hornsby (9) had more qualified seasons (with a .350+ batting average) than

Lajoie (6). He has the most seasons of 40+ doubles and 20+ stolen bases (7) all-time for second basemen.

So who was the best Nap/Indian of the first half-century of Cleveland baseball—Nap, or Shoeless Joe? Or neither?

The legendary "Shoeless" Joe Jackson, with his "Black Betsy" bat, 1913. (Charles M. Conlon)

The Rest of the Tribe

In 1915, the Indians traded both Lajoie and Jackson and put up just a 57–95 record.

*Enter **Tris Speaker**.*

Speaker was traded to the Indians in 1916 after batting .337/.414/.482 over nine years with Boston, and helped get Cleveland back to .500 (77–77). Over the next 10 seasons with Cleveland, Speaker put up a .354 average and an all-time franchise-best .444 on-base percentage.

Speaker ranks sixth all-time with a .345 career average. He was truly a contact king, once batting .489 for a month—July—in 1923, reaching base 81 times over 137 at-bats *without striking out once.*

Addie Joss batted .144 over his nine-year MLB career—but that's because he was a pitcher. Yes, during the Naps years, Cleveland actually had one of the game's best starting pitchers.

Joss owns Major League Baseball's second-best ERA all-time (1.89), pitching almost exclusively in the "Naps era" from 1902 to 1910. "The Big Train" Walter Johnson (six-foot-one), who broke in to the Big Leagues in 1907, might more accurately go by "The Caboose," as Joss (six-foot-three) was arguably the first "big man" to dominate the mound. Joss, with four complete individual seasons with a sub-1.75 ERA, is second only to Johnson, with eight.

Lou Boudreau was the MVP of the league, and team manager, when the Indians won their last World Series in 1948. The Hall of Fame shortstop had career highs in runs (116), hits (199), home runs (18), RBIs (106), batting average (.355), and probably high-fives (?) that year.

Incredibly, he struck out just nine times that season, averaging 75.1 plate appearances per strikeout, a mark no one has bested since. [Fun perspective: Tony Gwynn's career best mark was one strikeout per 38.5 plate appearances in 1995. Boudreau nearly doubled that during his MVP season.]

Bob Feller was one of the best young pitchers baseball had ever seen, winning more games in his teenage years than any other pitcher in the Modern Era (31, aged seventeen to nineteen—14 more wins than runner-up Dwight Gooden). He began a sharp career decline, though, at the age of twenty-nine in 1948, going 19–15 with a 3.56 ERA after his previous eight-year average of 19–9 with a 2.91 ERA. He averaged just 11 wins per season in his thirties.

Bob Feller had led the league in wins each season from 1939–41. He was up for a new contract. Instead, he signed on with the Navy and was the first American pro athlete to enlist in WWII. (US Navy Photograph)

Amazingly, Feller led all of baseball with 1,174 strikeouts from 1939 to 1946, despite serving in the US Navy for over three years, from December 1941 to August 1945.

Jim Thome and **Manny Ramirez** were two of baseball's brightest stars of the past 20 years, and got their start with Cleveland.

Both players played their first full season in 1995 for the Indians, and were nearly identical in their ability to dominate for a long period of time. Ramirez batted .319 with a 36-homer average and 1.017 OPS in six full seasons with Cleveland, while Thome batted .293 with 38 homers per season and a 1.013 OPS for seven full seasons with the Tribe.

Thome hit 337 of his 612 career home runs with Cleveland, while Ramirez knocked out 236 of his 555 career homers with the Indians. Babe Ruth and Barry Bonds (107 each) are the only players in baseball history to have had more games with both a home run and a double than Thome (99) and Ramirez (97).

STATS INCREDIBLE!

0: The home run total of Nap Lajoie in 1906. His 170 OPS+ that season easily tops Sammy Sosa's 63-homer 1999 campaign (151) and is the highest of the modern era for any player with zero home runs.

.402: Shoeless Joe's combined batting average through 1911–12.

114: Joe Sewell's impossibly-low strikeout total during his 14-year MLB career, spent mostly with Cleveland. The Hall of Fame shortstop owns the lowest career strikeout percentage of all time (1.4%; minimum 3,000 PAs).

1,075: From May 14, 1923 to May 26, 1930, Joe Sewell played 1,075 consecutive games without multiple strikeouts. He totaled just 54 strikeouts in 4,744 plate appearances during that time.

4.6: Francisco Lindor's WAR in 2015, the highest by an Indians rookie since Sewell in 1921. He's the first rookie shortstop with double-digit home runs, stolen bases, and defensive runs saved since Nomar Garciaparra in 1997.

6: The amount of Indians batters with a qualified .397+ on-base percentage. The Boston Beaneaters last had six such batters in 1894.

13: Jim Thome's career walk-off home run total, a major-league record. He's the only player in history to have his 500th home run be a game-ender.

612: Thome's MLB-leading home run total among left-handed batters/right-handed throwers.

72: The amount of double-digit K games tossed by Indians pitchers in 2014, a major-league record. In 2015, Cleveland had an MLB record five pitchers with a 9.5+ K/9 (minimum 50 innings). They are in a tie for this feat with four other teams: the 2015 Dodgers, 2014 Marlins, 2013 Mariners, and 2003 Cubs.

9: The number of times in MLB history that a team has had three pitchers with more than one strikeout per inning over 100+ innings. The Indians have done it the past three seasons.

8.888: The 2014 Indians averaged 8.888 strikeouts per nine innings in 2014—the most by a team in baseball history. The 2015 Indians averaged 8.839 strikeouts per nine innings, second best in baseball history.

7.0: Corey Kluber and Michael Brantley (2014) became the first Indians pitcher/position player combination since 1920 to each have at least 7.0 WAR.

200: In 2015, Corey Kluber and Carlos Carrasco became the first Indians teammates with at least 200 Ks each since Sam McDowell and Luis Tiant in 1968.

.397: Six different members (Vizquel, Lofton, Justice, Alomar, Thome, and Ramirez) of the 1999 Indians had an OBP of at least .397, the most on a team since 1894.

325: Kenny Lofton had 325 stolen bases, compared to just 324 strikeouts, from 1992–96.

DETROIT TIGERS

Est. 1901

Ty Cobb won the American League Triple Crown in 1909.
He batted .377 with nine home runs and 107 RBIs. All
nine of his home runs were inside-the-park.

The Detroit Tigers, the AL's oldest one-city, one-name team, began in 1894 as part of the Western League, a minor league that would eventually become the major American League (1901) we know today. Those formative years as a minor league franchise perhaps prepared Detroit for quick success in the majors, as the Tigers earned three straight trips to the World Series by 1909.

Detroit wouldn't win its first championship until 1935—of four world titles to this point—but, historically, it has been a steady franchise. Detroit is one of just six current American League teams with an all-time record over .500 (9,085–8,806, .508; behind the Yankees, Red Sox, and Indians, respectively). The addition of Ty Cobb in 1905 certainly spurred the Tigers to long lasting success.

The Georgia Peach played his first 22 years in Detroit, and for most of that period—at least until Babe Ruth's offensive game exploded in 1919—he was, arguably, the greatest hitter the game had ever seen. With an MLB-best .366 lifetime average, one could argue Cobb's might have been the game's sweetest stroke.

The Cobb era ended in 1926, but Hank Greenberg and Mickey Cochrane carried the offensive torch for the Tigers into the 1930s

(1935 champs) and lefty ace Hal Newhouser dominated the mound to help Detroit take a title in 1945. Lean years would follow, but from 1961–89 the Tigers would average 86 wins (excluding the strike-shortened 1981), and take two more championships (1968, 1984).

Right hander Denny McLain and catcher Bill Freehan were probably the best battery in team history, and played with, undeniably, the greatest player who sounds like a battery in Al Kaline (apologies, Doug Nickle). Thankfully, the Hall of Fame outfielder didn't play in today's media-centric era, or similar bad jokes and puns would follow Kaline like a lithium ion on a positive electrode.

No worries; the Tigers already have a modern day marvel in Miguel Cabrera. Miggy, a Triple Crown winner in 2012 (.330, 44 HRs, 139 RBIs), may be the franchise's greatest hitter since . . .

Ty Cobb

Cobb's reputation is that of a mean, abusive, hateful bully. To what degree is speculative, but clearly there is enough evidence to suggest Cobb was not an easy fellow to get along with.

His .366 lifetime batting average is still tops in baseball history, and at the time of his retirement in 1928, he was leading a slew of offensive categories as well, including hits (4,189), extra-base hits (1,136), and runs scored (2,244). His home run total (117) is scant by today's standards, but home runs would not become an important part of the game until the end of the Deadball Era and the emergence of the Babe in 1919. Consider:

Cubs slugger Sammy Sosa hit 66 home runs in 1998, and Cobb hit just 65 during a 13-year stretch in which he won 12 AL batting titles (1907–19)—finishing in the top seven in all of baseball in homers four times in that period, including a home run crown in 1909. Overall, Cobb actually had more league top-ten finishes in home runs (11) than Mark McGwire (10) and Ken Griffey Jr. (9).

Home run totals aside, the stats and feats of Tyrus Cobb's tremendous career are incredible:

- Seven seasons with at least 200 hits and 45 stolen bases are the most in baseball history. No other player even has five such seasons.
- Every year from 1907 to 1919, Cobb had a higher batting average than the league slugging percentage. He then did it again in 1922, during baseball's third season of "Live Ball" play, besting Babe Ruth and the rest of the American League .401 to .398.
- Was the first player to record consecutive .400 batting average seasons (1911, 1912), and maintained a .402 average over a four-year stretch from 1910 to 1913.
- At age thirty-nine in 1926, his final season in Detroit, Cobb batted .339 and struck out just twice in 273 plate appearances. He closed out the season with 59 straight games without a strikeout—a streak that extended another 19 games into the next season, when he was forty.
- In 2014, Astros second baseman Jose Altuve became just the second player ever to record 225 hits, 55+ extra-base hits, and 55+ stolen bases in a single season. Ty Cobb accomplished this in 1911 ... and 1912 ... and 1917.
- He would have to resurrect, return to baseball, and go 0-for-2,530 for his career batting average to fall below .300.
- Pete Rose eclipsed Cobb for the top all-time hits total (4,256 to 4,189), but, in terms of WAR, one full season (162 games) played by Cobb is worth about 361 played by Rose.
- Cobb has 16 qualified seasons with at least a .350 batting average. No other player has 10.
- Rickey Henderson had a 189 OPS+ with 65 stolen bases during his 1990 MVP campaign. The only other player with at least that was Cobb, who did it three years in a row (1909–11).

A gifted baserunner with a keen eye at the plate, Cobb was base-ball's most complete pre-Live Ball Era player. (*Sliding:* National Photo Company, 1924; *Standing:* Bain News Service, 1910.)

Cobb's career covered 79% of Detroit's MLB franchise existence upon the time of his retirement from baseball in 1928, but, over the years, there have been plenty of players that have helped define the franchise and share the spotlight.

Tiger Greats

Hank Greenberg was one of the first Tigers to follow Babe Ruth's lead out of the Deadball Era and into the age of prolific long balls.

He only played nine full seasons (minimum 400 at-bats; eight seasons with Detroit), but made his mark, exiting with a franchise-leading 306 homers—67 more than any other Tiger. He is still third on Detroit's all-time list, which is remarkable considering he lost all or most of four seasons serving in World War II.

Every season seemed like a gem for Greenberg, who certainly made the most of his relatively short Hall of Fame career.

In 1935, Greenberg led the league in homers (36) and RBIs (168), while leading the Tigers to their first ever World Championship.

In 1937, he set a record for RBIs (184) by a right-handed hitter that still stands, and reached 280 runs produced—a mark that hasn't been topped since.

His 58 home runs in 1938 are not just a team record—they are a record for the entire *modern* AL Central division.

In 1940, Greenberg (.340, 41 HRs, 150 RBIs) was just .012 away from the batting title, and the franchise's second Triple Crown. The *Quadruple* Crown is ambiguously defined, but Greenberg was close to a version of that as well, leading the AL with 50 doubles.

Greenberg was selected to serve in the United States Army on May 7, 1941, but was discharged a few months later on December 5, 1941. He would voluntarily re-enlist in the US Army Air Forces after Japan bombed Pearl Harbor and serve until July 1, 1945, when, after nearly four years, he led the Tigers to a World Series Championship. And despite missing four and a half of his prime seasons serving his great country, he is one of just six players in history with a career .600+ slugging percentage.

Al Kaline shouldn't get lost in the mix of such early talent in Tigers history, as he, too, was a dominant figure for the franchise.

He got off to a fast start, becoming the youngest player (20), to win a batting title (.340), besting Cobb by one single day.

Kaline didn't put up a ton of big, gaudy single season numbers—by his own admission, he "was never meant to be a superstar." However, the 10-time Gold Glove winner and 15-time All-Star spread his production out well through a 22-year career spent entirely in Detroit (1953–1974), amassing club records in home runs (399) and walks (1,277) that still stand today.

Of course, not all the best Tigers played over fifty years ago, and not all of them were hitters.

Hal Newhouser, one of those old timers, should probably be a more recognizable name, but his dominance as a starting pitcher was in perhaps too short a period of time.

Amazingly, in three full seasons from 1944 to 1946, Newhouser averaged a record of 27–9 and a 1.99 ERA. Sandy Koufax, during his three infamously dominant Cy Young seasons, averaged a 26–7 record with a 1.94 ERA. Hal led the AL in wins all three seasons, winning the Triple Crown in 1945 (25 Ws, 1.81 ERA, 212 Ks). Both pitchers won a Triple Crown in their respective stretches, but Newhouser one-upped Koufax, winning two MVP awards to Koufax's one.

Justin Verlander (24 Ws, 2.40 ERA, 250 Ks) was the most recent Tiger to pull off the rare feat of a Triple Crown and an MVP from the pitching mound in 2011, and did so on the 100th anniversary of Cobb winning the first ever AL MVP in 1911. In 2009, Verlander became the first qualified pitcher in team history with more strikeouts than innings pitched.

For an encore, **Miguel Cabrera** (.330, 44 HRs, 139 RBIs) won both the Triple Crown and MVP on the offensive side in 2012. In terms of OPS+, it was only his fifth-best season.

Since Cabrera joined the Tigers in 2008, he's batted .326 while averaging 34 home runs, 115 RBIs per season. No other American League player during that eight-year span has had even a SINGLE season that good.

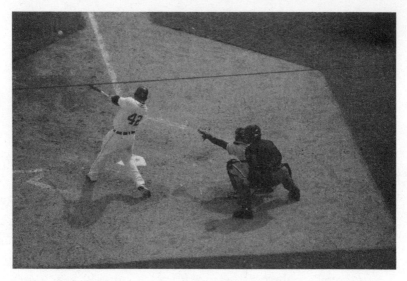

Miguel Cabrera, against the Chicago White Sox, ripping one of 34 home runs in 2009. (Kevin Ward, CC BY-SA 2.0)

STATS INCREDIBLE!

.402: Second baseman Placido Polanco's batting average after an 0-2 count in 2007.

117: Ty Cobb's career home run total. Babe Ruth hit 123 home runs just against the Tigers.

4: In 672 plate appearances in 1917, Cobb struck out just 34 times. One pitcher was responsible for four of them— Boston's ace, Babe Ruth.

.380: (Ty who?) Outfielder Harry Heilman's batting average from 1921–27, leading to four batting titles.

50%: In 1937, first baseman Rudy York hit 18 of his 35 home runs (51.43%) in August; in 1943, he hit 17 of his 34 homers (50%) in August.

.524: Miguel Cabrera's slugging percentage in 2014, his lowest season slugging since 2004 when he was twenty-one. The 2014 percentage was still good for 10th-best in baseball that year.

13: Miguel Cabrera batted .321/.399/.562 (155 OPS+) with 1,445 RBIs through his first 13 seasons. Henry Aaron batted .317/.375/.564 (156 OPS+) with 1,432 RBIs through his first 13 seasons.

75/75: Cobb's 79 extra-base hits and 83 stolen bases in 1911 make him the only man with 75+ XBH and 75+ SB in the same season.

3: In 2013, Detroit had three 200+ strikeout pitchers (Justin Verlander, Max Scherzer, Anibal Sanchez), tying the record for most in a season (1967 Twins, 1969 Astros).

1: Second baseman Charlie Gehringer's strikeout total in 90 career World Series plate appearances.

11: Number of Tigers players with double-digit home runs in 2004—a major-league record, since tied by the 2015 Houston Astros.

32/42: Catcher Victor Martinez had 32 home runs and 42 strikeouts in 2014. No other player in Tigers history had more home runs and less strikeouts in the same season.

KANSAS CITY ROYALS

Est. 1969

From 2014–15, Wade Davis became the first pitcher in baseball history with a sub-1.00 ERA over the span of two seasons (with at least 100 innings pitched).

2015 World Series champions!

Lately, the Kansas City Royals have been the undisputed best of the American League, but they've been dominating in such anonymity. They finally broke through in 2014, reaching the World Series after an unfathomable 28-year playoff drought, and then returned in 2015 to take the MLB crown. Their top hitter and pitcher, in terms of 2015 WAR? Outfielder Lorenzo Cain, and reliever Wade Davis. Not exactly names that resonate like Mickey Mantle and Whitey Ford.

In 2015, the Royals won a league-best 95 games, despite finishing just sixth in the AL (of 15) in runs per game (4.47), seventh in OPS (.734), third in ERA (3.73) and sixth in WHIP (1.282). They've managed to win more playoff games since dealing superstar Zack Greinke (22 wins; traded in 2010), than the three teams—Brewers (0), Angels (5), and Dodgers (8)—he has since played for, combined (13).

These World Series champions will always be linked with the 2015 club, but it was truly two years in the making.

To put it mildly, 2014 was a breakout year for the Royals. After an unfathomable 28-year playoff drought, the Royals finally broke through to the MLB postseason. And what a post-season it was.

The San Francisco Giants just narrowly edged the American League champion Royals, 3–2, in Game 7 of the World Series. Though they came up a hair short, the 2014 KC squad restored honor to the proud 47-year-old franchise.

In the beginning, the Royals were fast learners. The upstart franchise, named after the American Royal, a livestock and rodeo show in Missouri, eclipsed .500 in just its third season (85–76, 1971), and reached three straight AL Championship Series (1976–78) by the time it had logged a decade in KC.

The team averaged 90 wins per year from 1975–85, excluding the strike-shortened 1981. The common denominator of the seven playoff appearances and one championship in that span was the great George Brett (1.023 OPS in postseason play), but a lot of great players passed through Kansas City—just never enough to get back into contention.

Until . . .

2014

Wade Davis had the greatest win-loss percentage (.818; 9–2) in team history, and did so entirely out of the bullpen. Despite pitching just 72 innings on the season, Davis's output was historically dominant.

Davis's 109 strikeouts were the most without surrendering a home run since 1919 (Walter Johnson, 146 Ks). Aside from Davis and Johnson, who did it twice (also in 1916), only two other players recorded 100+ Ks without surrendering a home run in a single season over the past 100 years: Terry Forster (1972) and Babe Ruth (1916). Yup, the Babe was a heck of a pitcher, too.

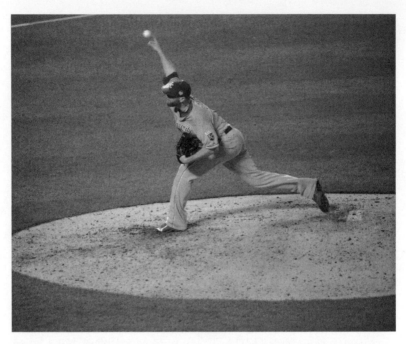

Wade Davis releasing the final pitch of the 2015 World Series. (Arturo Pardavila III, CC BY 2.0)

Davis and bullpen mate Kelvin Herrera became the first teammates to pitch at least 70 innings each without surrendering a home run since Lefty Williams and Reb Russell of the Chicago White Sox matched the feat in 1918.

The dynamic KC duo also became the first teammates EVER to each toss at least 70 innings, record a 20.0+ K% (strikeouts per plate appearance), and allow zero home runs—and this is even true since the innings-pitched minimum dropped to 20!

Not surprisingly, Kansas City's pitching staff was the story of its 2014 season, registering the franchise's second-best team ERA since 1986 (3.51; 3.45, 2013). Great pitching and a little good fortune helped Kansas City become the first team in MLB history to win three consecutive playoff games in extra innings.

The 2015 squad, for the most part, picked up right where it had left off the season prior. Davis never skipped a beat, somehow dropping his 1.00 ERA in 2014 to 0.94 in 2015. In three seasons with the Royals, he has yet to give up more than two runs in any relief appearance. As a team, they shined brightest in the postseason.

First baseman Eric Hosmer led all postseason batters with 17 RBIs, and outfielder Ben Zobrist tied an MLB record with eight playoff doubles. Clutch play in all facets of the game helped Kansas City outscore their opponents by a cumulative 40 runs after the sixth inning of play in the 2015 playoffs (51–11; credit: Christopher Kamka, CSN Chicago).

The Kansas City Bretts

George Brett played 21 seasons in Major League Baseball, all of them with the Royals. Even though he retired in 1993, he is still widely considered the face of the franchise.

Brett is currently the franchise leader in hits, home runs, RBIs, doubles, triples, (deep breath) runs scored, walks, games played, plate appearances, and All-Star Game appearances. Just to name a few.

Overall, glory years have been slim outside of Brett's tenure with the team, but it shouldn't detract from the amazing things he was able to accomplish with the Royals.

Brett (1979) and Jim Bottomley (1928, St. Louis Cardinals) are the only players in MLB history to hit 40+ doubles, 20+ triples, and 20+ home runs in a single season.

George Brett's statue on display inside Kauffman Stadium.
(Flickr Mr.Konerko, CC BY-SA 4.0)

In his 1980 MVP season, Brett (.390, +.1252) had the highest batting average above the MLB average of any recorded since Ted Williams (+.1306) in 1957. Tony Gwynn (.394, +.1241) was a close second in 1994.

Speaking of most valuable—the Royals were 73–40 (.646) with Brett in the lineup in 1980, and just 24–25 (.490) without him that year.

From May 8 to May 13, 1976, Brett had six consecutive three-hit games, batting .692.

Good company: Brett, Lou Gehrig, Roberto Clemente, Stan Musial, and Robin Yount are the only one-team players with 400+ doubles, 100+ triples, and 200+ home runs.

Since 1920, only Stan Musial (44) had more 3-for-3 games than Brett (40).

STATS INCREDIBLE!

5: 2015 rookie outfielder Paulo Orlando (great name) was the first Live Ball Era (1920+) player with five triples through his first seven career games. No other player even had four.

36: The Royals' single season home run record. Not by Brett, Hal McRae, Frank White, Mike Sweeney, or Carlos Beltran. Career .229 hitter Steve Balboni set the mark in 1985.

28: Herrera did not allow a single earned run in the eighth inning in 2014. His 28 (eighth) innings are the most ever by a reliever with a 0.00 ERA.

2,287-to-1: The Royals threw 228,700% more 97+ MPH pitches in 2014 than the Minnesota Twins.

1st: 2014 rookie hurler Brandon Finnegan became the first player to pitch the College and MLB World Series in the same year.

0.97: Wade Davis's ERA from 2014–15. It is the lowest ERA for a pitcher over a consecutive season span.

9: Davis's career World Series innings pitched. He allowed zero earned runs, six hits, zero walks, and 18 strikeouts.

1: The lone plate appearance (a strikeout) for rookie Raul Mondesi in 2015 came during Game Six of the World Series. He became the first player to debut in the championship series since Cincy's Bug Holliday on October 17, 1885.

MINNESOTA TWINS

Est. 1901

Torii Hunter, who played 12 of his 19 seasons in Minnesota, had 353 home runs, 195 stolen bases, and 9 Gold Glove Awards in his career. Only one player, Willie Mays, had more of each.

The Twins franchise is a tale of two cities, and no, that's not a weak play on their namesake derived from the "Twin Cities" of Minneapolis and St. Paul. Rather, it's a weak play on all of that, mixed with the fact that they have actually played more seasons as a franchise (60 to 55) in Washington, DC, as the Senators.

Founded in 1901 as one of the original eight teams of the American League, the Senators were lousy their first 11 seasons of play, compiling just a .377 winning percentage, with an average record of 55–92. Then, Walter Johnson (career Senator, 1907–27) helped change everything for the team, blooming into one of the game's all-time greatest hurlers, and carrying the Senators into respectability at a time when continued failure could have spelled the end for baseball in Washington.

They eventually won their lone championship in the DC era in 1924, Johnson's MVP season. After a short stretch of success in the 1930s, the Senators were dreadful again—so dreadful, people referred to Washington as "first in war, first in peace, and last in the American League." In fact, they were so dreadful that someone made a movie about it (*Damn Yankees*, 1958). In fact, the Senators got so bad for so long, they had to pack up and leave.

The team that found itself in Minnesota in 1961, dubbed the Twins, actually showed glimmers of hope. The Senators managed just five +.500 seasons in their last 25 years in Washington, but they had a young Harmon Killebrew in tow, and enjoyed the best of his Hall of Fame seasons in Minneapolis.

The Twins wouldn't win a title until 1987 (and again in 1991), but with the contributions of Killebrew, Rod Carew, Burt Blyleven, Kirby Puckett, Johan Santana, and most recently Joe Mauer, they've been a consistent contender across multiple decades.

Past meets future, as former MVP Joe Mauer meets AL Rookie of the Year candidate Miguel Sano at home plate in Baltimore, 2015. (Keith Allison, KeithAllisonPhoto.com)

The Big Train

When you look back, Walter Johnson (417–279, 2.17 ERA) was so good for the Senators, it kind of makes up for how terrible the whole stretch in Washington was.

Johnson is the only pitcher to win the AL pitching Triple Crown (league leader in wins, ERA, and strikeouts) three times, and owns 20% of all such seasons in American League history.

In 1924, at the age of thirty-six, he won a championship, his second league MVP award, and his last Triple Crown, which, along with 23 wins and 158 strikeouts, included a 2.72 ERA. A sign of the times—the Big Train didn't have an ERA above 2.22 in any of his 13 pitching-friendly, Deadball Era seasons.

In a ten-season stretch from 1910–19, Johnson averaged 27 wins and a 1.59 ERA. The American League has not seen a *single* season ERA champion with an ERA that low since Johnson himself finished with a 1.49 in 1919.

Walter Johnson averaged 34 complete games over a seven-year period, from 1910–16. Zack Grienke has only once ever made 34 starts in a single season. (Charles Conlon)

He is one of just four players over the past 100 seasons (including Babe Ruth) to pitch at least 250 innings in a season without surrendering a home run, and he did it twice (1916, 1919). In each of those seasons, Johnson managed a home run of his own, with a whopping 369.2 innings pitched in 1916.

So adept at keeping the ball inside the park, Johnson actually had more career complete game shutouts (110) than home runs allowed (97). Randy Johnson, just during the stretch in which he won four straight Cy Young awards (1999–02), surrendered 98 home runs. Walter Johnson is still the most recent player with 200+ strikeouts and zero home runs allowed in the same season (1916) and the only pitcher to lead the majors in strikeouts without allowing a home run since Candy Cummings danced his way to the feat in 1875—again, doing so twice, in 1916 and 1919.

Classic Twins

Harmon Killebrew ushered in the Twins age with a bang—475 bangs in a Minnesota uniform, to be exact (573 homers in all, including 84 in Washington and 14 in Kansas City).

Killebrew accrued the third-most home runs in MLB history (272) through 1,000 career games, behind only Ryan Howard (279) and Ralph Kiner (277).

He retired in 1975, but, on the Twins franchise (Senators included) single-season home run list, Killebrew still ranks first, second, third, fourth, fifth, sixth, t-seventh, ninth, and t-tenth.

Playing alongside Killebrew for the first nine years of his career, fellow Hall of Famer **Rod Carew** was the perfect complement, with a completely different style.

Carew had a smooth stroke that led to a .328 career batting average, but only 92 home runs. He is the Twins' single season (9.7, 1977) and career (63.7) WAR leader, and the single season (.388, 1977) and career (.334) batting average leader.

In 1977, Carew batted .401 at the halfway point. He finished at .388, but with 16 triples and 23 stolen bases, he became the first .380/15/15 man since George Sisler in 1922, and no one has done it since.

We rarely see it today, but of his 19 stolen bases in 1969, seven were steals of home.

A hybrid of the thunder and lightning combo that was Killebrew and Carew, **Kirby Puckett** led the charge toward Minnesota's last two championships (1987, 1991). A fan favorite who helped put a spotlight on baseball in Minnesota, Puckett was a career Twin, playing 12 seasons before bowing out due to injury. He won six Gold Gloves, played in 10 straight All-Star Games, and is second to only Carew in team batting average in a Twins uniform (.318).

Puckett was drafted by the Twins with the third pick in the January part of the 1982 draft, and finished his career with a 50.9 career WAR. The rest of the players selected in the first round that year finished with a combined WAR of -0.7.

No Walking in Minneapolis
Two pitchers in Twins history have pitched recently with absurdly accurate results.

From August 3, 2003 to May 10, 2007, a time spent mostly with the Twins, right-hander Carlos Silva made 99 consecutive starts without surrendering more than two walks.

In 2005, he was superhuman, recording the best single season K/BB ratio (7.89) of any pitcher with less than 100 strikeouts since 1884. To put it in perspective, consider: On May 5, 1970, Twins great Luis Tiant walked nine batters in a single five-inning start. Silva walked nine batters in 188 innings for the *entire 2005 season*.

Phil Hughes may have upped the ante in 2014, walking just 16 batters in 209.2 innings. He registered an 11.63 K/BB ratio that season, the best qualified mark since Candy Cummings (20.5) in 1875, when nine balls were required for a walk.

Silva's 2005 is the best BB/9 innings ratio in baseball's modern era. In fact, the only pitchers in the game history to best that mark played during a time when eight or nine balls were required for a walk; most recently George Bradley accomplished the feat in 1880.

STATS INCREDIBLE!

.358: The Twins were 29–52 on the road in 1987, the year they won the championship.

0: The Twins were on the good and bad side of two of the greatest World Series Game 7 pitching performances of all time—Sandy Koufax's three-hit shutout of Minnesota in 1965 for the Dodgers, and Jack Morris's 10-inning 1–0 shutout of the Braves in 1991. Twins great Tony Oliva was blanked by Koufax in the first game, and was Minnesota's hitting coach for the second.

127.5: Walter Johnson's JAWS (a Hall of Fame–worthiness value statistic, see page 265). The only other players over 100 are Cy Young (123.8) and the man who won the most Cy Young awards, Roger Clemens (103.3).

18: Innings pitched by Johnson in a complete-game shutout of the White Sox on May 15, 1918.

200: The 1967 Twins are one of just three teams (1969 Astros, 2013 Tigers) to have three pitchers with 200+ strikeouts (Dean Chance, Jim Kaat, Dave Boswell).

3: The number of no-hit bids Joe Mauer has ended in the ninth inning.

.365: Joe Mauer's batting average in 2009, the highest batting average in baseball history by a catcher with at least 100 games caught in a season. His .444 OBP was *only* third best—Mickey Cochrane topped it in 1935 (.452) and 1933 (.459).

13th: Johan Santana's place on the all-time career K/9 list (8.83). He only has one qualifying entry on the single season top 100 (41st, 10.46).

41: The amount of games it took rookie Miguel Sano to hit his first 10 home runs in 2015, making Sano the fastest player to 10 homers in franchise history.

9: Double plays by Torii Hunter, from 1999 to 2001. He committed just eight errors over the same span.

6: During his six-year peak from 2003–08, Johan Santana had a 156 ERA+ with 9.4 K/9. The same ERA+ and K/9 that Hall of Famer Sandy Koufax registered during his five-year peak from 1961–66.

96: Rod Carew could have gone an additional 0-for-96 and still won the AL batting title in 1977.

AMERICAN LEAGUE WEST

HOUSTON ASTROS

Est. 1962

In 1994, Jeff Bagwell became the first player to slug .750 or better in a season with at least 15 stolen bases since Babe Ruth in 1923. The only other such season in baseball history? Babe Ruth, again, in 1921.

The Astros began as the Colt .45s as part of MLB expansion in 1962. The name and logo, though cool and probably inappropriate, would be short-lived, as everything was re-branded Astro-centric in 1966 in an homage to the Houston center of the NASA space program. The team became the "Astros"; the mammoth new dome stadium, coined the Eighth Wonder of the World, became the Astrodome; even the new synthetic turf, which made its debut in Major League Baseball that year, transitioned from "ChemGrass" to "Astroturf."

The team struggled out of the gate, with over half of the franchise's worst 13 seasons occurring in its first seven years of play (1962–68, .418 W–L%). The uniforms were routinely colorful and cool, even now as a retro-hipster throwback, but that's really all the team had going for it until the 1980s.

Probably not coincidentally, the Astros' first postseason appearance came in 1980, after the offseason acquisition of Nolan Ryan. Ryan had established himself in eight prior seasons with the Angels as one of the hardest-throwing, hardest-to-hit power pitchers in the game's history. It was an important turning point, as the Astros had begun to define their franchise from the pitching mound.

Ryan (1980–88, 3.13 ERA), Bob Knepper (1981–89, 3.66), Mike Scott (1983–89, 3.19), and Joe Niekro (1980–85, 3.18) solidified the Astros rotation for much of the decade. The 1985 and 1988 Astros were the only two squads in the '80s to have four starters with at least 20 quality starts.

First baseman Jeff Bagwell and jack-of-all-trades Craig Biggio headlined the "Killer B's" offensive eruption for the 'Stros in the 1990s and 2000s, culminating in the franchise's only World Series appearance in 2005 (L, 4–0 vs. Chicago White Sox).

In 2015, the 'Stros made their first playoff appearance since that World Series loss in 2005. They improved by 16 games on the season prior (86–76) behind a strong core of young talent. They didn't advance beyond the ALDS, but that's the Houston way! The team is certainly on the rise, and, like those of the Killer B era, very exciting to watch.

Win or lose (the big one), Ryan's age-defying 100-MPH heater, Bagwell's gravity-defying crouching tiger–stance at the plate, and those gloriously-ugly uniform machinations have helped make *style over substance* an ever-enticing proposition in Houston.

The Ryan Express

Nolan Ryan, at 3.13, is the Astros' franchise leader in ERA (minimum 800 innings). He overwhelmed hitters with power, striking out more batters (1,866) than any other Astro. It was his resiliency over time, however, that made this strikeout artist a legend.

Ryan came from the California Angels having won seven of the previous eight AL strikeout titles, with the single-season strikeout record in tow (383; 1973), but it was with Houston that Ryan proved his skills were seemingly impervious to aging.

His age thirty-seven to forty seasons with Houston, Ryan actually improved his WHIP from 1.218 to 1.185 over his age thirty-three to thirty-six seasons. Ryan's final two seasons with Houston, aged forty to forty-one, he actually posted a better ERA (3.15), WHIP (1.191), and K/9 (10.4) than his age thirty to thirty-one seasons with California (3.19/1.374/10.1).

He's only the fourth pitcher of the modern era to lead the league in ERA as a quadragenarian (2.76), joined by fellow Astro Roger Clemens, who in 2005 became the oldest player in MLB history with a qualified ERA under 2.25 (1.87, turned forty-three in August that season).

The Killer B's

In 1996, the Astros acquired third baseman Sean Berry to add to their offensive core of Jeff Bagwell, Craig Biggio, and Derek Bell. They finished in the top six in WAR that season, and the "Killer B's" was born (and used ad nauseam on SportsCenter). Really, the Killer B's had just two consistent members—Bagwell and Biggio.

Jeff Bagwell *(1B, 1991–2005)*: A career Astro, he's Houston's all-time leader in WAR (79.6), OPS+ (149), home runs (449), and RBIs (1,529). And he did it all while sitting down on the job—sort of.

Bagwell was diabolical throughout the 1990s in how he subliminally convinced a small-but-potent faction of youth baseball players that a batting stance should begin as though you're sitting on a tiny, invisible chair. He was crouched so low, looking so impossibly silly, one could wonder if the whole thing was part of an elaborate double-dog-dare. But, it worked.

Bagwell put up two seasons (1997/99) with 30+ doubles, 40+ home runs, 30+ stolen bases, and 100+ walks. The other 18,000+ players in MLB history have never done that once. During his career (1991 through 2005), Bagwell led all of baseball with 2,597 runs produced.

Jeff Bagwell's impossibly low crouch. (Barbara Moore, CC BY-SA 2.0)

Craig Biggio *(C/2B/OF, 1988–2007):* The Hall of Fame second baseman is the only player in baseball history with an All-Star nod at both catcher and second base, and also played significant time in center field (288 games). He's the only player in MLB history to play at least 200 games as a catcher, middle infielder, and outfielder, but it's what he did in the batter's box that really set him apart.

A lifetime, 20-year Astro, Biggio leads the franchise by healthy margins in hits (3,060), runs scored (1,844), and total bases (4,711). He was a pesky batter, and a furiously tough out, leading baseball's modern era with 285 hit-by-pitch walks. Add sac flies and sac bunts to that number, and Biggio "sacrificed" his body or his at-bats more times than any other player during the Live Ball Era (467; post-1919).

And then there was **Lance Berkman** *(OF/1B, 1999–2010).* Though not an original "B," Berkman was a buzzworthy addition to the club from the onset, hitting a rookie record 21 homers in

2000. He sits third in club history in runs scored (1,008), total bases (3,053), and RBIs (1,090) behind the original B's, but the stat that made him a real pain in the "b" for opposing pitchers? Among switch-hitting, left-handed throwers, Berkman's 366 career home runs are an all-time record.

Up the Middle

The Astros have a bright future, thanks to one of the best young middle infields in the game.

Second baseman Jose Altuve (age twenty-five, .313 BA, 15 HRs), in his fifth season, reached 830 hits in just 668 career games through last season. Hit King Pete Rose had just 800 through as many games. Altuve led the league in stolen bases for the second

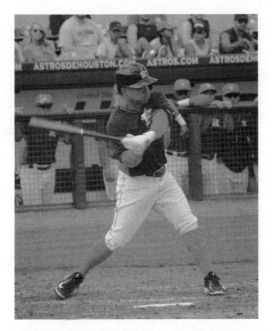

Jose Altuve, 2015. (Eric Enfermero, CC BY-SA 4.0)

straight year (38) and was the shortest player (five-foot-six) with consecutive 200-hit seasons since Willie Keeler from 1894–1901.

Rookie Carlos Correa (age twenty, .279 BA, 22 HRs) had a 4.1 WAR on the year, becoming the youngest shortstop with a WAR that high since John McGraw in 1894. In the postseason, Correa debuted as the youngest shortstop to start a postseason game since Travis Jackson in 1924, and became the youngest at his position to hit a home run, knocking one out against the Royals in the ALDS.

On one special night, the duo shined, becoming the first Astros double-play combo each with a multi–home run game in the same game (10/26/2015), and the first DP pair overall to pull off the feat in 15 years.

They're not B's—there's not a single B in either of their names (*stats!*), but early on, they've been a killer combination for Houston.

STATS INCREDIBLE!

8: Carlos Beltran's (another B!) home run total through his first nine career postseason games with the Astros in 2004. Over 12 games that postseason overall, Beltran batted .435 with 14 RBIs.

16: The number of wild pitches thrown by Nolan Ryan in 1981, with a 1.69 ERA. In the modern era, it's the lowest ERA by any player who led the league in both categories.

220: The amount of batters that Roy Oswalt faced after an 0–2 count in 2006. He walked none of them.

.824: Oswalt's W–L% in 2001 (14–3), making the Wizard of Os, twenty-three, the youngest rookie in NL history with a winning percentage over .800.

225: In 2014, second baseman Jose Altuve became the shortest player (five-foot-six) in baseball's modern era with a 225-hit season.

285: Times Biggio was hit-by-pitch during his career, effectively raising his career on-base percentage from .348 to .363.

6: Number of Astros batters with 100+ strikeouts and fewer than 50 extra-base hits in 2014, the most on a team in baseball history. They repeated the feat in 2015.

14: Jeff Bagwell totaled 446 home runs through his first fourteen career seasons—one more than Barry Bonds had through his first fourteen seasons.

331: In 1999, Bagwell reached base safely 331 times—the most by a right-handed batter in baseball history.

0: In 1997, Craig Biggio led the NL with 744 plate appearances. He grounded into *zero* double plays (78 chances).

228: Billy Wagner had 228 more strikeouts than baserunners allowed during his career, the largest differential of all time.

LOS ANGELES ANGELS OF ANAHEIM

Est. 1961

Mike Trout played 652 games during his first five seasons. He batted .304/.397/.559 (169 OPS+) with 37.9 WAR, 139 home runs, and 113 stolen bases. Through his first five seasons, Mickey Mantle played 658 games, batted .298/.400/.528 (155 OPS+) with 29.7 WAR, 121 home runs, and 33 stolen bases.

The Angels have always seemed to be a team at war with itself. They began as the Los Angeles Angels (1961–64), playing most of their home game games at Dodger Stadium. By 1965, they switched to the all-inclusive *California* Angels, tweaked to account for their thirty-one-mile move southwest in 1966, to Angel Stadium in Anaheim, California. From 1997 to 2004, they shifted to the aesthetically-agreeable *Anaheim* Angels, before ruining a great thing, and taking up their current moniker, the *Los Angeles Angels of Anaheim*. Which is kinda silly.

Legally, the team must maintain a tie to Anaheim in the names of its club and stadium. And that's a noble stipulation, considering the Halos have called Anaheim home—while not always *literally* calling it home—for the past 50 years. Alas, as the new saying goes, "home is where the desired demographic market size is," and LA is primed to be siphoned for the otherwise-unrepresented American League.

Surely, that kind of waffling naming history speaks of internal struggles within the franchise—and that may well be because of the team's external struggles against the rest of Major League Baseball.

Through the Angels' first 40 years, they reached the postseason on just three occasions (1979, 1982, 1986 ALCS losses), never playing in a World Series. Two of the team's top players over that span were Chuck Finley (1986–99, 52.2 WAR) and Jim Fregosi (1961–71, 45.9). Despite still being franchise WAR leaders, they combined for just five Hall of Fame votes (of 807) at the close of their careers.

Things abruptly turned around for the franchise in 2002, as the team reached, and won, its first World Series, to start a competitive run that, really, has yet to let up. Prior to their championship season, the Halos had never won more than 93 games in a single year, but over an eight-year stretch, from 2002–09, the team averaged 93 wins per season, reaching the postseason six times—twice as many times as they had in the entire twentieth century. They've averaged "just" 86 wins per season from 2010 to 2015, but a return to dominance seems inevitable.

Twenty-four-year-old wunderkind Mike Trout, who, in four full seasons, has never finished lower than second in MVP voting, is signed with Anaheim through 2020. Wherever, and whatever, they call home, the Angels have never been on more solid ground.

Los Angeles, California

It would be accurate to categorize the twentieth century of Halo baseball as "lean years." To gloss over those four decades, however, would be inappropriate. Sure, the Angels are one of five teams without a player representative in the Hall of Fame, but some all-time greats still put up memorable seasons for the Halos before the turn of the century.

Jim Fregosi *(SS, 1961–71)*: Fregosi is perhaps best remembered for his managerial career that spanned four decades, but, during his playing days, he was one of the game's best shortstops.

Fregosi was the only AL shortstop during the 1960s to bat over .264 (.270; minimum 3,000 PAs), and was the only shortstop in baseball over that span with a cumulative WAR over 37 (37.4). He finished second or third among AL shortstops of the decade in hits (1,160), OPS (.741), doubles (171), and walks (450).

Various injuries prevented a potential Hall of Fame finale for Fregosi. Following the worst statistical year of his career (.233/.317/.326), the six-time All-Star was shipped to the New York Mets in an historically lopsided deal that landed California the Strikeout King...

Nolan Ryan *(SP, 1972–79)*: The Ryan Express hadn't really picked up steam until joining the Angels in his fifth full season in the big leagues. While Ryan inexplicably dons a Rangers cap on his Hall plaque, he had far more All-Star appearances (5), wins (138), and strikeouts (2,416) with the Angels than with any other team. Among power pitchers, he enjoyed one of the most dominant stretches in baseball history.

In just his first six seasons with California, Ryan led the league in strikeouts five times, fanning over 300 batters each time. Walter Johnson (2), Steve Carlton (1), and Pedro Martinez (2) combined for just five career 300-K campaigns, despite 63 years of MLB service between them.

In 1973, he bested Sandy Koufax's modern era strikeout record by one, recording 383 Ks in a single season. He led the league with 23 double-digit strikeout games (the entire LA Dodgers team finished a distant second, with just 15). Ryan's 15 games with a dozen or more strikeouts in 1973 are the most in baseball history.

Just 13 players have recorded a 300+ strikeout season during the entire Live Ball Era (post-1919). Ryan averaged 302 Ks during his eight years with the Angels.

Nolan Ryan, holding the baseball from his record-breaking 383rd strike-out of the 1973 season. (Jon Rogers Collection, PD)

Rod Carew *(1B, 1979–85):* Carew is in the Hall as a Minnesota Twin, but he was fantastic in his six seasons with California to close out his career. The five-time Halo All-Star sits second among Angels in career batting average and on-base percentage (.314, .393, respectively).

At thirty-seven years old in 1983, Carew was batting .500 as late as May 6th, and .400 as late as July 15th. He finished up at .339, hitting .402 in his first 268 plate appearances, and just .273 in his final 268.

Despite low home run totals, Carew was feared by the opposition. He had five qualified seasons with the Angels in which he had more intentional walks than home runs. His 12 total—along with his seven with the Twins—are the most since the intentional walk officially became a statistic in 1955.

Jim Abbott *(SP, 1989–92, 1995–96):* There were a few other players that have come along in major-league history that played while having just one hand (Pete Gray, 1945; Chad Bentz, 2004–05), but Abbott was, by far, the most talented and accomplished.

Being born with no right hand was no insurmountable obstacle for Abbott, who entered the pro baseball league highly touted, secured by the Angels with the eighth overall pick in the 1988 draft.

In 1991, Abbott finished third in AL Cy Young voting (18–11, 2.89 ERA), putting up the second-best pitching WAR for the Angels since 1977 (7.6). Over a two-year stretch, from 1991–92, Abbott was truly one of the best pitchers in the American League, finishing second to only Roger Clemens in ERA (2.83, minimum 350 IP).

After a trade to New York, Abbott did pitch a no-hitter for the Yankees in 1993, but he was never as dominant as he was his prior two seasons with the Angels. After a return to California, Abbott actually had one of the worst full-season pitching performances ·ever.

Abbott pitched to a 2–18 record in 1996, with the highest ERA ever recorded in AL history (7.48, minimum 140 IP).

Never matter. Abbott's abilities far outshined his apparent disability on the baseball diamond, and he remains one of professional sports' most enduring, and endearing, heroes.

The Resurrection

Given the franchise's bleak history prior to the twenty-first century, the only thing perhaps more impressive than the Angels' seemingly out-of-nowhere World Series run in 2002 has been their ability to maintain that success over time. Some of the best players of this era have played major roles in keeping Anaheim on top over the past 14 years.

Garret Anderson *(OF, 1994–2008)*: Anderson is one of just two players (Darin Erstad) with the Angels through the team's last three name changes, but he played his best baseball in 2002 and 2003.

Anderson led the Halos offense in 2002, and the American League in doubles (tied with Nomar Garciaparra with 56). It was only the third 55+ doubles season in the AL since 1936. With an

AL-leading 49 doubles in 2003, Anderson became just the second player in league history (Edgar Martinez; 1995–96) with consecutive seasons batting .300+, with 25+ home runs and 49+ doubles.

Vladimir Guerrero *(OF, 2004–09)*: In 2017, Vlad may be enshrined in the Hall of Fame—and rightfully so. It will be the first strong case to be made for an Angels cap in the Hall.

While Vlad's numbers were marginally more gaudy with the Montreal Expos, he won his only MVP with the Angels in 2004, and led Anaheim to the postseason in five of his six seasons with the club—something he never did once in Montreal.

Vlad had four seasons with at least 200 hits and 30 home runs (2004 and 2006 with Anaheim), trailing only Lou Gehrig, who had seven such seasons in his Hall of Fame career. With tremendous bat control and unparalleled range in the batter's box, Vlad is the only player since Stan Musial in 1963 to finish his career with over 400 home runs and less than 1,000 strikeouts.

Albert Pujols *(1B, 2012–)*: Technically, Pujols is still a member of the 400+ HR/ sub-1,000 K club, but he's got six years left on his contract with Anaheim to rack up the paltry 22 strikeouts required to oust him. While he's nothing close to the player he once was, he's likely far from finished.

Pujols was one of the best players to ever put on a uniform while with St. Louis. In his 11 seasons as a Cardinal, he averaged 40 home runs and 121 RBIs. Reggie Jackson never recorded a single 40+ HR/ 120+ RBI season in his entire career.

The Anaheim iteration of Pujols has yielded much different results. In his four seasons with the Angels, Pujols has averaged just 29 home runs and 92 RBIs, while seeing his batting average drop from .328 in St. Louis to .266 in Anaheim. Still, his 40 home runs were good for fifth in the AL in 2015, and, at thirty-five years old, made him the oldest right-handed batter to slug at least 40 home runs in a season since Mark McGwire hit 65 in 1999.

If he can match that power output in 2016, Pujols (thirty-six) will be the third-youngest player to reach 600 home runs, behind only Alex Rodriguez (thirty-five) and Babe Ruth (thirty-six).

Mike Trout (OF, 2011–)

What Pujols was for St. Louis, that's what **Mike Trout** has been for Anaheim. If Vlad doesn't beat him to it, Trout sure seems like a shoo-in to be the first Angel enshrined in baseball's Hall of Fame.

Where to start? Trout led the league in runs (129), stolen bases (49), and OPS+ (168) his very first full season in the big leagues (2012), cruising to Rookie of the Year, and finishing runner-up for MVP. He secured the MVP hardware two seasons later, in 2014, leading the league in runs (115), RBIs (111), and total bases (338).

Already, at twenty-four years of age, Trout is measuring up to the game's all-time best . . .

- Trout is tied with Willie Mays for the most seasons (2) with at least a .320 batting average, 25 home runs, and 30 stolen bases all-time.
- Only Babe Ruth (5) and Barry Bonds (10) have more seasons during the Live Ball Era with at least a 165 OPS+ and 10 stolen bases than Trout's four.
- In 2014, he became the first player to lead the American League in runs, RBIs, and strikeouts since Babe Ruth in 1923.
- He has more career seasons with at least a .550 SLG and 15 SBs than Mickey Mantle has—three to two.
- He has more career seasons with at least 65 XBHs and 65 BBs than Joe DiMaggio—four to three.
- Trout has three seasons with at least a 9.0 WAR—more than Pujols, Rickey Henderson, Ken Griffey Jr., Cal Ripken Jr., and Hank Aaron, to name a few.
- He is already tied with Mays in career top-two MVP finishes—more than Aaron and Griffey Jr. combined.

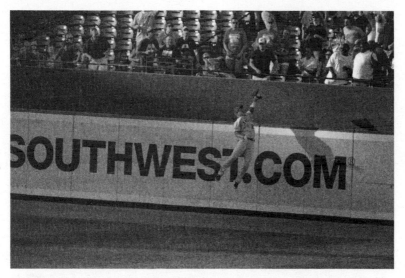

Mike Trout, taking a home run away from J. J. Hardy of the Orioles in 2012. (Keith Allison, KeithAllisonPhoto.com)

STATS INCREDIBLE!

3: Times Nolan Ryan struck out at least 19 batters in a single game in 1973, an MLB record. Only Randy Johnson (1997) even had two such games in a season.

58: Red Sox batters faced by Ryan on June 14, 1974. He struck out 19 and walked 10 in a 13-inning no-decision. He threw 278 pitches, and struck out leadoff man Cecil Cooper six times. The Angels won, 4–3, in the 15th.

1983: The year Angels representative Fred Lynn hit the first, and only, grand slam in the history of the All-Star Game.

70: The 2000 Angels are the only team in MLB history with three 70+ extra-base hit outfielders (Darin Erstad, Garret Anderson, Tim Salmon).

0.79%: Percentage of players in baseball history who have both more home runs and stolen bases than twenty-four-year-old Mike Trout.

9.42: Trout's WAR per-162 games, second only to Babe Ruth (10.57).

.287: Trout's batting average in 2014 was the lowest for an AL MVP since Harmon Killebrew batted .276 in 1969.

3: Seasons Trout accumulated 325 total bases and 75 walks—one more than Derek Jeter and Mike Schmidt, combined.

6: The number of players in the American League's 115-year history to hit a walk-off grand slam while trailing by three runs, with two outs. Angels shortstop Dick Schofield was the fourth to pull the trick, giving the Angels a 13–12 win over the Tigers on August 29, 1986.

32.8: Number of strikeouts per home run allowed by starting pitcher Garrett Richards in 2014, the best ratio by a qualified pitcher since Pedro Martinez in 1999 (34.8 K/HR).

OAKLAND ATHLETICS

Est. 1901

In 1981, Rickey Henderson, at the age of twenty-two, stole 56 of 78 bases during his first tour with the Athletics. In 1998, Rickey Henderson, at the age of thirty-nine, stole 66 of 79 bases during his third tour with the Athletics.

2022 will be a big year for the Oakland Athletics. That marks the year that their tenure in Oakland will top the franchise's 54-year tenure in the City of Brotherly Love.

All but forgotten, the Athletics had an extremely successful run in Philadelphia, winning five championships over nearly six decades. By city, that total ranks them behind only the New York Yankees (27), St. Louis Cardinals (11), and Boston Red Sox (8). So, why the move? The A's, among the most successful franchises in professional sports to change locations, were historically up-and-down.

Established in 1901 as a charter American League franchise, the Athletics of Philadelphia were owned and managed by Connie Mack for its first 50 years. While Mack was known for shrewd moves, like poaching crosstown Phillies players—most notably Nap Lajoie in 1901—he was also quick on the trigger to unload his rosters and tank seasons. From 1910 to 1914, the A's averaged 98 wins, and appeared in four World

Series, winning three. In 1915, they finished last, with 43 wins, and the 14th worst record in the history of baseball's modern era. The following season? Thirty-six wins and a .235 winning percentage—the worst record since 1886, at a time when flat-sided bats were fair play and handlebar mustaches were practically a requirement.

Team photo of the Philadelphia A's first World Series appearance, 1905. Featured, most notably, is manager Connie Mack, "The Tall Tactician" (center, suited), and his star pitcher, seated to his right, Rube Waddell. (Boston Public Library, McGreevey Collection)

All in all, the Philadelphia A's finished with five championships, despite an unremarkable .477 win percentage. With the NL Phillies making the World Series in 1950, capturing the city's fans at a critical time, the Athletics became a Philly also-ran and were exiled to Kansas City by 1955.

The franchise's 13 years in KC are mostly forgotten because the team never really got close to .500 during any season. By comparison, the Athletics' first 13 seasons in Oakland, starting in 1968, featured a run of three straight World Series titles and an 84-win average—ten more than their best finish in Kansas City. The Athletics had found their home.

Hall of famers Reggie Jackson, Rollie Fingers, and Catfish Hunter led the A's dynasty of the 1970s, cementing the franchise's standing in California. Since, the A's won their final title in 1989, led by Mark McGwire and Dennis Eckersley, and have averaged 86 wins per season since Billy Beane took over the GM position in 1998.

Oakland still has seven years and two championships to go to top its Philadelphia past, but the franchise has never been on more solid ground.

The $100,000 Infield

John McInnis (first base), Eddie Collins (second base), Jack Barry (shortstop), and Frank Baker (third base).

That was the Athletics' starting infield from 1911–14 that reached the World Series three times, winning titles in 1911 and 1913. The "$100,000 Infield" moniker was a distinction of the quartet's market value, and Connie Mack's willingness to splurge when the timing was right. Barry was a serviceable shortstop, but the stars were Collins, Baker, and McInnis.

"Cocky" Collins: His .333 batting average is 26th all-time, and .337 average over 13 seasons with the A's is third in franchise history. Notoriously selective at the plate, Collins (1,031) is one of just three players in MLB history with 1,000 more walks than strikeouts (Ted Williams, 1,312; Barry Bonds, 1,019).

Solidly entrenched in the Deadball Era, Collins (5 WAR per season average) had 16 seasons in which his WAR was at least double his season home run total. Barry Bonds, in all but one of his 22 seasons, had home run totals at least TRIPLE his WAR.

"Home Run" Baker: He was the Babe Ruth of the Deadball Era. Baker led the league in homers his last four years with the Athletics (1911–14), totaling just 42 over that span. In 1921, Baker's first season playing with the Babe, Ruth hit 42 homers just through his first 100 games. Baseball historian Bill James called Baker's time with the $100,000 Infield (.334 BA/30.9 WAR) "by far, the greatest four-year stretch by a third baseman in baseball history."

"Stuffy" McInnis: The lone non-Hall of Famer of the trio, McInnis had a career that seems to beg for enshrinement.

His 20-home run total over 19 years is very low for a first baseman, even in the Deadball Era, when the league single-season record stood at just 16. But, aside from leading all first basemen in fielding percentage six times, his *small ball* bat was among the very best in the game during the 1910s.

During the decade, McInnis batted .300 over more seasons (7) than any other first baseman in baseball. Over the span of his career (1909–27), McInnis recorded 13 seasons with more walks than strikeouts, more than any other player at his position. And he's one of just 12 players during the modern era to average 30+ at-bats per strikeout for his career.

The New Bill James Historical Baseball Abstract ranks each of the 1912 through 1914 $100,000 Infield seasons among the top five infields in the game's history.

Jimmie Foxx

One of the most gifted hitters of all-time, Jimmie Foxx spent half of his Hall of Fame career in Philadelphia in the 1930s putting up numbers that had scarcely been matched in the game's history, before or since.

Foxx debuted at the age of seventeen with Philly in 1925, and from his first at-bat to his last, 20 years later, Foxx never at any point had his career batting average dip below .325.

In 1932, Foxx had the most hits of any player in a 50+ home run season (213 hits, 58 HRs). His .364 batting average is the highest for a 50+ homer season by anyone not named "Babe" in baseball history.

Only four players have ever batted .350+ with 45+ home runs and 140+ RBIs in the same season. Foxx *averaged* .350 with 46 home runs and 144 RBIs over a four-year stretch with the A's from 1932–35.

The Bash Brothers

During the late 1980s, the Deadball Era was long-forgotten and the home run was king.

First baseman Mark McGwire and outfielder Jose Canseco played together for seven seasons with the Athletics (1986–92), winning a title in 1989. A spoof on the "Blues Brothers" film, the duo was referred to as the *Bash Brothers* as an homage to their tremendous home run power.

[Note: It's impossible to bring up these two without mentioning their connection to PEDs (performance-enhancing drugs). Along with Barry Bonds, they are the primary poster boys for the Steroid Era drug problem during a 15+ year span in Major League Baseball. We acknowledge it happened, and we don't condone the use of PEDs, aside from the Flintstones Chewables variety. That being said, home runs are awesome, so let's try to have a little fun with this.]

During their time together with the A's, aside from being the best power-hitting duo on one team, they were the top two home run hitters in all of baseball. From 1986 to 1992, no one hit more homers than McGwire (220) and Canseco (230; 4 with Texas in parts of 1992).

Jose Canseco *(OF, 1985–92, 1997)*: From the depths of stat obscurity, it can—and should—be noted that, in 2014, White Sox slugger Jose Abreu broke Canseco's records for home runs by a Cuban-born rookie, and home runs by all rookies named Jose (36 to 33).

In a more conventional statosphere . . .

In 1988, Canseco became the first member of the 40–40 club, hitting 42 home runs and stealing 40 bases, but he wasn't classically fleet of foot, averaging just 12 swipes per season over his career, from 1985 to 2001. What he did well, though, he did great—over that span, no one in the American League hit more than Canseco's 462 home runs.

Mark McGwire *(1B, 1986-97)*: Big Mac set the power bar high early on in Oakland, establishing a new rookie record for home runs with 49 in 1987. Slugging .618, McGwire was one of just two rookies in American League history with a slugging percentage over .600 (Rudy York, 1937; .651).

Compared to his Bash Brother, or really any other of the game's greatest sluggers, McGwire was a true one-trick pony. While Canseco averaged 12 steals per season, McGwire stole a total of just 12 bases during his *entire 16-year career*. He hit 583 home runs, 10th-most in MLB history, while accumulating just 252 doubles—654th most in MLB history. His six career triples are half the amount Babe Ruth had in one season in 1919 . . . while pitching for the Boston Red Sox.

All-time, Mac had the the most seasons with twice as many home runs as doubles (10), but it's unfair to pile on his one-dimensional production. The one-trick Clydesdale slugged and walked himself to the 9th-best OPS of all-time (.982).

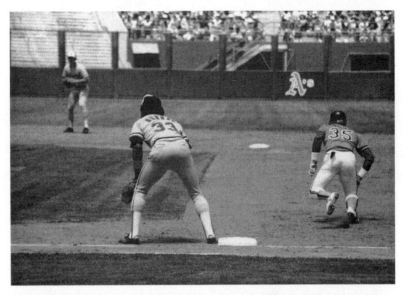

Rickey Henderson, taking off to steal one of his MLB-best 103 bases in 1983. Hall of Famers Eddie Murray (1B) and Cal Ripken (SS) man the infield for Baltimore. (Gary Soup)

STATS INCREDIBLE!

349: Starting pitcher Rube Waddell's strikeout total in 1904 that stood as an American League record for 69 years (383; Nolan Ryan, 1973).

4: The amount of times the American League has had a new single-season strikeout record. Waddell set the first three.

16: The American League single-season home run record, set in 1902 by A's outfielder Ralph "Socks" Seybold, that stood until Babe Ruth took the crown with 29 in 1919. A's second baseman Nap Lajoie established the original mark with 14 in 1901.

33: Outfielder Reggie Jackson's home run total through his first 71 games of 1969—a 74-homer pace. He finished with 47.

41: MLB record for consecutive relief appearances without issuing a walk, set by A's bullpen ace Dennis Eckersley from August 17, 1989 to June 10, 1990.

18.33: Eck's K/BB in 1989. Best by a pitcher with at least 50 strikeouts since Candy Cummings in 1875—when nine balls were required for a walk.

23.97: The amount of miles covered by Rickey Henderson while stealing his MLB record 1,406 bases.

10/100: Rickey Henderson had 10 home runs and 130 stolen bases with Oakland in 1982. He's baseball's only 10/100 man, and the first 10/90 player since Harry Stovey in 1890.

75.3: Lou Brock's career stolen base percentage. Henderson had a 79.6 SB% after breaking Brock's all-time stolen base record.

189/65: Henderson had a 189 OPS+ with 65 stolen bases in 1990. The only other player with at least that in a season was Ty Cobb (1909–11).

4: Singles hit by Mark McGwire on September 20, 1987—the only four-single game of his career.

4,000: On July 18, 1927, with the Athletics, Ty Cobb hit a double against his former team, the Detroit Tigers, establishing the 4,000 hit club.

SEATTLE MARINERS

Est. 1977

Only seven players in baseball history have bested each leg of Edgar Martinez's career .312/.418/.515 slash line. It is a roll call of MLB legends: Ted Williams, Lou Gehrig, Rogers Hornsby, Babe Ruth, "Shoeless" Joe Jackson, Dan Brouthers, and Jimmie Foxx. In fact, David Ortiz matched each leg of Edgar's career slash line just ONCE in a season (2007).

Seattleites must be a patient bunch.

The Mariners have been around for 39 years and have finished over .500 just 12 times. Meanwhile, the Yankees haven't finished *under* .500 since right around the time DVDs were invented (1995). The Mariners have never won a World Series, or even appeared in one, so their fans still haven't gotten their hands on one of those *Sports Illustrated* championship DVDs. Still, it hasn't been all doom and gloom in Seattle.

After 12 straight losing seasons to start the franchise, the stars aligned for Seattle—literally. In 1989, outfielder Ken Griffey Jr. was called up and future ace Randy Johnson arrived via trade, bringing together two of the greatest players of the next generation of Major League Baseball.

Both players made their All-Star debuts the following season, and by 1991, had helped Seattle finally break .500 (83–79). With Alex Rodriguez added to the mix full-time, and Edgar Martinez emerging as baseball's premier DH, by 1996, the once-forlorn franchise had a gluttony of riches . . . and a window.

During the 10 years Griffey, Johnson, and Martinez played together (1989–98), the Mariners finished over .500 five times and won the division twice (1995, 1997). But, looking back, the Mariners' opportunity to win a championship was mostly confined to just the two-year stretch, with A-Rod, from 1996–97, when the quartet of superstars were at the peak of their Seattle powers.

Of the four, only Rodriguez and Martinez remained by 2000, and the Mariners still won a franchise-best 91 games. The following year, A-Rod was replaced by a Japanese Pacific Leaguer. The team upped the ante and won an AL-record 116 games. Over any four-year stretch during the 2000–10 decade, only the Yankees (100 Ws, 2001–04) averaged more wins than the Mariners (98 Ws, 2000–03).

While, as of the start of the 2016 season, Seattle hasn't reached the playoffs since 2001, Mariners history has proven that turnarounds can be swift and mighty. Reinforcements always seem on the way, and the next batch could make Seattle's long, bumpy road very much worth the wait.

Junior

Ken Griffey Jr. was a lauded nineteen-year-old phenom when he started with the Mariners in 1989. The anticipation soon gave way to monstrous expectations, as "The Kid" spent significant time in the 1990s as the face of baseball, and *the chosen one* to take the home run, and all of baseball, to new heights. Of course, this was overblown.

It's easy to look at Griffey's career for what might have been if he was able to stay healthy and take a crack at Hank Aaron's then-home run record (755 career HRs). But then, you're cheating the career that actually *was . . .*

During the 1990s, Griffey led all of his American League contemporaries in home runs (382) and runs scored (1,002), earning an All-Star nod and Gold Glove each season. Judged historically, Griffey was just as special:

- Had five seasons—four of which were consecutive, from 1996–99—with at least 45 home runs and 15 steals, which is just one fewer than those of every other Hall of Famer combined.
- Twice had 55+ home run/ 15+ stolen base seasons, matching the total of all other major-league players in history. His 56 home runs/ 20 stolen bases in 1998 make Griffey the only 55/20 player ever.
- Hit more home runs in the month of May than any other player (134). Mr. May is also the single-season home run champ among center fielders, hitting 56 in both 1997 and 1998.
- Among outfielders, only Willie Mays had more consecutive seasons as an All-Star and Gold Glove winner (12 to 10).
- From September 19, 1995 to July 14, 1998, Junior batted .305/.389/.653, averaging 60 home runs and 157 RBIs per 162 games played.

Griffey, looking little, awaits a pitch in 1997. (Flickr Clare_and_Ben, CC BY-SA 2.0)

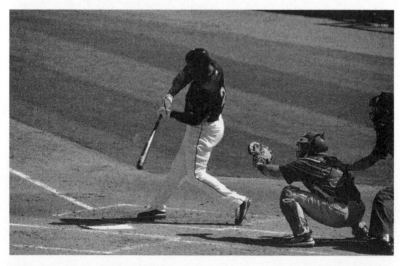

Like most power hitters of the '90s, Junior had a lot more bulk on him by the end of his career, ca. 2009. (Jeff Corrigan Sports Photography, CC BY-SA 3.0)

Edgar

Historically, designated hitters have had a difficult time gaining enshrinement in baseball's Hall of Fame. Chicago's Frank Thomas is routinely considered the first, and only, primary DH to enter the Hall (2014), but he still played 42% of his 2,322 career games at first base. Edgar Martinez (DH, 1987–2004), meanwhile, played just 29% of his 2,055 MLB games in the field—a sticking point that may well be his sole barrier toward enshrinement. Looking back on his brilliant career, though, it's clear his bat was exceptional—and a worthy exception to the unwritten rule that's been keeping him out.

Martinez was a late-bloomer, clubbing 264 home runs with 1,057 RBIs after age thirty (of 309 HRs, and 1,261 RBIs for his career). He reached base safely 2,369 times in his thirties, for a .4360 on-base percentage—just slightly ahead of Ty Cobb in his thirties (2,341 TOB, .4357 OBP). Only 13 players in baseball history have a better career OBP than Martinez (minimum 7,000 plate appearances). One of them is Barry Bonds, and the rest are all Hall of Famers. The next three players ranking below the slugger are also in the Hall.

During a three-year stretch, from 1995–97, Martinez's teammate, Ken Griffey Jr., compiled a stout .385 OBP. Martinez topped it during the same stretch with a .386 . . . with two strikes against him.

Martinez had two seasons with at least 25 home runs, 50 doubles, and 110 walks (1995–96)—the same number of seasons that every other player in MLB history had *combined*. That's really rare company. And he has just three years left of Hall ballot eligibility to prove he belongs with some of the rarest talents in the game's history.

While current Boston legend, David Ortiz, is getting buzz as, arguably, the greatest DH of all-time, and a shoo-in Hall of Famer, it's important to note that, in terms of career WAR, one full season (162 games) played by Edgar Martinez is worth about 241 games played by Ortiz.

The Big Unit

It's hard not to snicker at the notion that a man named *Randy Johnson* could be nicknamed "The Big Unit" and neither is an adult film alias. Actually, the nickname supposedly originated from teammate Tim Raines exclaiming that Johnson was "a big unit" his rookie season in Montreal. Until Jon Rauch (six-foot-eleven) debuted in 2002, Johnson, at six-foot-ten, was the tallest player in the game's history. Looking back on his Mariners career, he was also one of the most talented.

In 1989, his first season with Seattle, Johnson had a career-worst 18.2 K%, which was still a better rate than Jim Palmer's three Cy Young seasons. For his career, the strikeout artist K'd 28.56% of the batters he faced, the most ever by a qualifying pitcher. Nolan Ryan, the all-time strikeout leader (5,714 Ks), would have to un-retire and strike out 1,050 straight batters to pass Johnson in career K%.

Johnson led the league in ERA (2.48) and strikeouts (294) during his Cy Young 1995 season, but his 18–2 record was historically unique. It is the best win percentage (.900) in the American League since 1937. Taking his three-season totals from 1995–97, Johnson managed a remarkable 43–6 record, for an .878 win percentage, the highest three-year percentage in modern baseball history (minimum 70 games). Over a single season, only four AL pitchers were able to top the percentage that Johnson maintained over three years.

The Unit reached even higher heights, dominating the regular and postseasons while winning four straight Cy Youngs with the Arizona Diamondbacks, en route to Hall of Fame enshrinement in 2015. His premature departure is something Seattle fans hope doesn't repeat with their current ace, Felix Hernandez.

King Felix

It's not just a nickname—it's a reality for Seattle's star hurler. In 2015, Hernandez pitched his 11th season with Seattle, one more than Johnson. As such, he's managed to take Johnson's crown atop a slew of franchise pitching categories.

Felix currently leads the franchise in ERA (3.11), pitching WAR (49.8), and WHIP (1.171; minimum 1,000 innings), and needs two wins in 2016 to match Jamie Moyer's Seattle record (145). In stark contrast to Johnson, wins have been historically hard to come by for King Felix.

His 13 wins in 2010 were the lowest total ever for an AL Cy Young–winning season. He led the league with a 2.14 ERA in 2014, but had a remarkable 2.45 ERA and 0–6 record in games he *didn't* win that season. By the end of 2014, his 4.25 ERA in non-win starts was the lowest of the Live Ball Era (minimum 175 non-win starts). At thirty years old, he's already made 119 career starts with 0–2 runs in support—more than Pedro Martinez (110), and just a tad behind Curt Schilling (120) and John Smoltz (121). He has a 23–65 record and 2.93 ERA in those games.

Hernandez is the only pitcher in baseball history with 200+ strikeouts and 75 or fewer walks in at least six consecutive seasons (2009–14). He's signed through 2020, and will be looking to be king of the hill for the next Mariners postseason run.

STATS INCREDIBLE!

409/398: Alex Rodriguez (409) and Ken Griffey Jr. (398) hit the most home runs in MLB history before their thirtieth birthday.

4,924: Most hits by a father-son combo in MLB history. Ken Griffey Sr. and Jr. bested Bobby and Barry Bonds by 103.

174: Randy Johnson's ERA+ from 1994 to 2002. Felix Hernandez had a career-best 174 ERA+ in 2010. First-ballot Hall of Famer Tom Glavine had a career-best 168 ERA+ in 1998.

94: Double-digit strikeouts games for Johnson with the M's, a franchise record. The next seven closest in club history tallied 94 combined.

21.197: A-Rod was 21 years and 72 days old on the final day of the 1996 season. He batted .358/.415/.631 that season—the highest batting average, on-base percentage, and slugging percentage in a qualified season by a player his age or younger since Cap Anson (.415) in 1872, Al Kaline (.421) in 1955, and Mel Ott (.635) in 1929, respectively.

6: The amount of Mariners pitchers with more strikeouts than innings pitched in 2013 (minimum 50 innings), an MLB record.

0: Starter Hisashi Iwakuma became the first ever Tokyo native to toss a no-hitter in Major League Baseball.

2,142: Felix Hernandez is the all-time strikeout leader among Venezuelan-born players.

8: Times Junior homered on Opening Day (all with the Mariners). Adam Dunn also has 8 opening day home runs.

12: Number of players in baseball history who have at least 830 career extra-base hits with an on-base percentage of .415 or better. Ten of them are Hall of Famers. The other two? Edgar Martinez and Barry Bonds.

36,587: The number of pitches Ichiro has seen during his MLB career (through 2015), of which, only 25 have come while he did not have a lifetime batting average of .300 or better.

73: From June 23, 1995 to June 20, 1996, Edgar Martinez had 73 doubles over the span of 162 games. He even added two three-baggers!

0.5: Difference between Tony Gwynn's 68.8 career WAR and Martinez's (68.3). Only one was a first-ballot Hall of Famer.

179: Ichiro Suzuki's intentional walk total, ranking him 27th all-time, despite being 705th in homers (113).

2001: The year Ichiro became the first player to win a league batting title, stolen base crown, and Gold Glove Award in the same season. Dee Gordon (2015) is the only player to do it since.

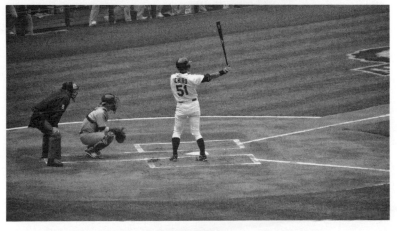

Ichiro's iconic batting stance, 2010. (Dave Sizer, CC BY 2.0)

TEXAS RANGERS

Est. 1961

Nolan Ryan had more complete game no-hitters (7) than complete game no-walkers (4) during his Hall of Famer career.

When the Washington Senators (Twins) split for Minnesota after the 1960 season, Major League Baseball moved up expansion and awarded the nation's capital a bright, shiny new team for 1961—the Washington Senators. The players and historical records were off to Minneapolis while just the name and penchant for losing remained. Washington had essentially traded in its old clunker for a brand new lemon.

Over 11 seasons in Washington, the Senators averaged a dismal 67 wins and 94 losses. Ownership and management, save for a very short-but-sweet managerial stint from first-timer Ted Williams, bumbled the operation from the onset and the team was sold and moved to Arlington, Texas, by the 1971 season.

The Rangers, named after Texas's statewide law enforcement agency, finished dead last the first two years in their new AL West digs, and wouldn't finish first in the division until 1994, a strike-shortened season with no World Series. But, it hasn't been all doom and gloom in the Lone Star State.

President Richard Nixon throws out the ceremonial opening pitch of the Senators' 1969 season. Washington manager Ted Williams, left, looks on. (Warren K. Leffler, *US News and World Report*, LOC)

In the mid-1970s, the Rangers were mixing-and-matching Hall of Famers with All-Star-caliber players in and out of the starting rotation. Gaylord Perry, Ferguson Jenkins, Burt Blyleven, and Dock Ellis never formed their own *super rotation*, but they all played a short-term role in bringing respectability to Texas from 1977–79, featuring a then-best 94–68 finish for the ball club in 1978.

A solid foundation of ownership mixed with a Texas-size level of enthusiasm and patience among the fan base has made the Rangers a team worth watching, and worth the wait. The Rangers broke through to the postseason in the late-1990s, made serious runs at the World Series in 2010/11, and that first championship seems closer than ever.

Nolan Ryan and the Two Towers

With the Rangers, **Nolan Ryan** was kind of like Gandalf from *Lord of the Rings*. He was really old (forty-two to forty-six), absurdly powerful (3.43 ERA, 10.1 K/9), and helped lead the way for two aspiring heroes (Ivan Rodriguez and Juan Gonzalez). Of course, it might not be polite to call "Pudge" Rodriguez the mightiest of Hobbits, and, sadly, rings were never part of the journey for the 1990s Rangers.

After helping the Astros reach new heights in the '80s, Ryan seemed to do the same for the Rangers in the '90s, signing in Texas for the 1989 season. He played there for five seasons in his forties, and dominated much of the time. He wasn't just great for his age . . . He was just great.

As far as quadragenarian power pitching starters go, Ryan is in a class of his own:

- He's the oldest pitcher to lead the league in strikeouts (forty-three years old; 232 Ks).
- In 1990, he became the oldest player in MLB history to lead the league in WHIP (1.034). The following season, at age forty-four, he set a new bar, pitching an AL-best 1.006 WHIP.
- He's the only qualified starting pitcher in baseball history, over age forty-one, to have a 10+ K/9 season—and he did it three times, 1989 through 1991, leading the AL each year (11.3, 10.2, 10.6, respectively).
- Of the 49 players over age thirty-nine to pitch a full season, Ryan and Randy Johnson are the only players to lead the league in strikeouts. Johnson, forty, did it once in 2004 (290 Ks). Ryan did it for four straight years from 1987–90.

Ryan pitched in Advil commercials into his fifties, but Major League Baseball is a whole different ballgame. After Ryan's final season in 1993, the torch was passed on to a new, offensive, generation of Rangers baseball.

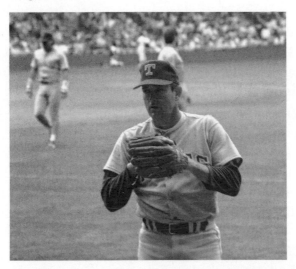

Geriatric, but historic. Nolan Ryan led the league in strikeouts his first two years with Texas. He was forty-two and forty-three years old. (Chuck Anderson, CC BY 2.0)

Juan González: Juan Gone was an immediate hit his first three full seasons in the majors, knocking in 102 runs in 1991, and leading the league in homers the following two seasons (43, 46, respectively). He missed parts of two seasons with Texas due to injury, but, even so, over an eight-year stretch (1992–99) he compiled a per-162-game average of 48 home runs and 146 RBIs. By comparison, career RBI leader Hank Aaron's best eight-year, per-162 stretch, was 45 home runs and 116 RBIs from 1966–73.

The shame of González's career is that, taken wholly, it seems unfinished. Steroid-use rumors aside, he was a great player that retired too early. Playing just one at-bat past age thirty-four, the two-time MVP finished with a higher home run percentage than Barry Bonds (6.07% to 6.04%).

Ivan Rodriguez: Pudge, like González, was great from the onset. He was an All-Star his first 10 full seasons, winning Gold Gloves each year. His progression as a hitter was profound, as his batting average improved from (*deep breath*) .260 to .273 to .298 to .303 to .313 to .321 to .332 to .347 over that span. Although he was one of the best hitting catchers in the game's history, his defense set him apart.

Rodriguez, tops in career WAR among Rangers (49.9), is also tops in career defensive WAR for the team (20.8) and owns the best dWAR mark overall among catchers in baseball history (28.7).

Of course, there were a lot of other players that had key roles in turning the franchise around in the '90s, including Will Clark, Ruben Sierra, and most notably, Rafael Palmeiro, the Rangers' career offensive WAR leader (40.6).

Post-2000

Before the 2001 season, the Rangers made headlines, signing Alex Rodriguez to an historic, 10-year $252 million contract. While the team didn't do well during the three years he served in Texas under the deal, individually A-Rod was a star, achieving the highest OPS+ of any Ranger in history.

He led the league in home runs all three seasons, and he's the only Ranger to eclipse the 50-homer mark, doing it in back-to-back years in 2001–02 (52, 57). Those two totals are the highest for any American League player having batted a full 162+ game season.

The 2010 and 2011 Rangers nearly powered their way to World Series championships, losing to the Giants and Cardinals, respectively, in the final showdown. Outfielder Josh Hamilton, an All-Star each season, was a big part of that success, especially during his 2010 MVP year.

Hamilton was one of just 13 players over the past 50 years to compile a .350+/ 30 home run/ 100 RBI season, going .359/32/100 in 2010. He's also one of just six players this millennium to bat

.350+ with a .625+ slugging percentage. In either case, no one has matched Hamilton's 2010 season since.

Third baseman Adrian Beltre joined the team as a free agent in 2011 after leading the league in doubles. Besides helping Texas repeat as AL champions that year, Beltre has been one of the most important additions to a Rangers team that has been consistently competitive ever since.

Since joining the team, no other third baseman in baseball has had as many .300 batting average seasons (3) or 30 home run seasons (3) as Beltre. Beltre has already built himself a Hall of Fame resume: he has a higher career WAR than Ken Griffey Jr. (83.8 to 83.6), he—along with Brooks Robinson and Roberto Clemente—is just one of three players in history with at least 2,000 hits, 200 homers, and 200 defensive runs saved, and he is the only player in history with at least 1,000 extra-base hits, 100 stolen bases, and 200 defensive runs saved.

STATS INCREDIBLE!

6: Complete games thrown by forty-two-year-old Nolan Ryan in 1989. Twenty-six-year-old Cy Young winner and NL MVP Clayton Kershaw led all of baseball with six complete games in 2014.

203: Batters that Ryan stuck out in 1991, while allowing just 183 total baserunners. He was forty-four.

1,283.2: Career innings pitched by ace closer Mariano Rivera, including 1,173 strikeouts and 998 hits allowed. Ryan recorded 1,437 strikeouts and just 933 hits allowed in 1,271⅔ innings pitched *after turning forty*.

2000: The year Rangers utility man Scott Sheldon became the only player in MLB history to play every position (including pitcher and DH), and bat in every spot in the lineup.

11: Intentional walks collected by Rangers first baseman Prince Fielder in 2014, one more than Miguel Cabrera. Fielder played just 42 games that year, while Cabrera played all but three.

3: The amount of All-Star team nods for starting pitcher Yu Darvish (2012–14), one for each season he's pitched in the majors. No other Rangers pitcher has made more.

616: Yu Darvish's strikeout total through 75 career games. He's the first player ever with over 600 through as many games.

200/50: Alex Rodriguez had 201 hits and 52 home runs for the Rangers in 2001. He was the first player with at least 200 hits and 50 homers in a season since Jimmie Foxx in 1932.

Also …

18: A-Rod's steals total that season, making him the first 200 H/50 HR/15 SB since Babe Ruth in 1921.

2.284: Cliff Lee averaged 2.284 strikeouts per *ball three* in 2010. The MLB average was 2.174 strikeouts-per-*walk* that season. His 10.28 strikeouts-per-walk was the best ratio by a pitcher with at least 200 innings since Candy Cummings in 1875, when nine balls were required for a walk.

198: Nolan Ryan had 198 career non-win quality starts. He was 0–107 with a 2.27 ERA, 1.166 WHIP, and 9.77 K/9 in those starts.

II. NATIONAL LEAGUE

NATIONAL LEAGUE EAST

ATLANTA BRAVES

Est. 1871

Hank Aaron homered at a rate of once every 13.08 plate appearances during his age thirty-seven to thirty-nine seasons. Barry Bonds homered at a rate of once every 13.08 plate appearances during his age thirty-seven to thirty-nine seasons.

The Braves are the oldest continuously operating team in baseball, founded in 1871—just seven short years before Edison's bright idea for the incandescent lightbulb.

They started out in Boston as part of the National Association before becoming a charter member of the National League in 1876. In the 25 seasons leading up to American League expansion of Major League Baseball (1901), the Red Stockings/Beaneaters held their own, finishing in first place eight times. But, that success would be short-lived.

In a situation similar to what happened in Philadelphia, between the Phillies and Athletics, the Beaneaters had some of their best players poached by the incumbent AL Boston Americans (Red Sox). Three of the Beaneaters' top five players, in terms of WAR, jumped to the Americans to start the 1901 season. The Americans' new tenancy would prove to have far-reaching consequences for their NL counterpart, but in the short-term, it just made the Beaneaters lousy.

They finished over .500 just once over the next 13 seasons, shifting team names between the Doves, Rustlers, and Braves in the process, proving superstition always had an illogical strangle-hold on America's pastime.

Their 1914 season is probably the sole reason why we call them the "Braves" today. That year, in one of professional sports' most dramatic turnarounds of all time, the Braves won the World Series over the Philadelphia Athletics, despite being in last place, at 26–40, in early July. They finished out going 68–19, blowing away the NL competition, and in turn, the A's for the championship. The success was sudden, and contained, but the effects were memorable. Over the next 33 years, the Braves would finish better than fourth place just three times. But hey—at least the name stuck. The city? Not so much.

The Braves actually had a short spurt of success in the mid-1940s, culminating in a losing effort to the Cleveland Indians in the 1948 World Series (4–2). The pull of greener pastures was too much, however, and by 1953, the Braves were Milwaukee-bound. And it was probably the greatest relocation in sports history.

In Milwaukee, the Braves set new National League attendance records in 1953, 1954, and 1957. The play on the field dramatically improved, as Hall of Famers Eddie Mathews (1953) and Hank Aaron (1955) each played their first (of 30 total) All-Star seasons for Milwaukee. The rest of baseball took notice, and the Braves' success would serve as the catalytic thrust behind the Athletics', Dodgers', and Giants' move out west, all within the same decade.

It's not a stretch to call the Braves "The Team that Hank Built," considering the Braves had their first really great run while Hank Aaron was at the top of his game. During the 14 straight seasons he led the team in WAR (1956–69), the Braves had just one sub-.500 season, with three first-place finishes, plus a World Series title in 1957.

The move to Atlanta wasn't performance-based—the Milwaukee Braves are still the only multi-year franchise to never have a losing record. It was entirely about money, and Atlanta was a much bigger market. The city fought hard to keep the team, but, by 1966, the Braves had a new permanent home.

The Braves fell back into a long stretch of mediocrity in Atlanta, reaching the playoffs just twice over a 25-year stretch. Then, they went out and won the division every year, from 1991 to 2005. Ho-hum. They made it look easy, dominating with a trio of Hall of Fame aces—Greg Maddux, Tom Glavine, and John Smoltz—and becoming a fixture in the MLB playoffs every single year for an entire generation.

[Consider: During their run, the Braves won their first division crown the same year the first web page was developed. Eighty-five or so million websites later, the Braves would finally relinquish the crown.]

It was an exciting era for the franchise, and it was loud about it, considering, at the time, Braves games were televised nationally on Turner Broadcast networks. They've reached the playoffs just three times in ten seasons since, but the sweet smell—*Mets fans read: stench*—of prosperity still wafts about Atlanta, like the residual fumes of a speeding race car, lingering long after the race is through.

Surely, the Braves won't be moving cities again any time soon. In 2017, they're slated to move into the new Sun-Trust Park—the house that success built.

Spahn & Sain

The Braves' brief mid-1940s spurt and 1948 Series run is often credited to the pitching arms of Warren Spahn and Johnny Sain. If the duo sounds familiar, it's most likely because of the poem that bears their name, nicknamed, "Spahn and Sain and Pray for Rain."

Reality, as is usually the case, tells a much different tale (see: *Tinker to Evers to Chance*).

Hall of Famer Spahn, a 14-time All-Star who led the league in wins eight times during his 21-year career, was inarguably amazing. He was, however, just breaking into the big leagues at this time, and the extent of his eventual 363-win greatness was far less defined.

1950 Braves rotation, featuring Warren Spahn (far right), and Johnny Sain (center) . . . Oh, yeah, and Vern Bickford, who led the league in complete games that season (27) and more than doubled Sain in pitching WAR (5.0 to 2.4). (Author unknown; *Baseball Digest,* March 1951)

In Sain's case, he had his three best seasons for the Braves during the team's only three winning seasons of the decade, from 1946–48. He averaged a 22–14 record over that span, with a 2.77 ERA, which is stellar. However, there was certainly no dramatic drop-off from there, and the Braves rotated in a slew of talented arms.

- In 1946, Mort Cooper had the third-best ERA on the team (3.12), and actually led the entire league in WHIP (1.106).

- In 1947, Red Barrett had somewhat of a statistically-identical season to Sain, with a 3.55 ERA, 111 ERA+, and 1.201 WHIP (Sain: 3.52/112/1.293).
- In 1948, the year attributed to the poem, Spahn actually finished LAST in the four-man rotation in ERA (3.71) and ERA+ (105).

No disrespect to Spahn, or Sain—they helped the Braves finish better than the league average in ERA, ERA+, and WHIP all three seasons, with Boston leading each category in 1948. But it was much more of a well-rounded, team effort.

Not aesthetically-pleasing, but, maybe try:

Spahn, Cooper, Barret, Sain . . . heck—just pray for rain.

Hammerin' Hank

Because of Hank Aaron's tremendous accomplishments, Eddie Mathews doesn't get his proper due—not even in the title of this section.

Aaron (755 HRs) would go on to break Babe Ruth's home run record (714 HRs), but during the 14 years the two sluggers played together, he only hit 47 more homers than Mathews (468 to 421). And actually, Mathews hit more before his thirtieth birthday than the champ (370 to 342).

Mathews was one of baseball's quickest studies, hitting the most home runs in MLB history before his age-twenty-four season (153; tied with Mel Ott). All-time, among primary third basemen, he sits behind just Mike Schmidt in homers (512), WAR (96.4), and OPS+ (143). Fitting that, no matter how you frame it, Mathews always ends up behind someone else in the end.

The aforementioned Aaron is, of course, the prime example.

Aaron had a stellar, 23-year MLB career, and ranks first all-time in RBIs (2,297) and total bases (6,856). Barry Bonds may be the current Home Run King (762 to Aaron's 755), but Aaron still owns a few less-extravagant home run records of his own:

> *Hammerin' Hank is the all-time home run champ for the months of June (150) and July (152), and he hit more at home than any other player (385). He had the most games with at least one home run (692) and the most games in which he homered without striking out in MLB history (485). He hit the most single-season homers for a player in his age-thirty-seven season (47; 1971), and the most in a career before age forty (713).*

Of course, it's not all about home runs with Aaron. He had more career RBIs than Hall of Famers Ralph Kiner (1,015), Rod Carew (1,015), and Wade Boggs (1,014) *JUST IN GAMES IN WHICH HE DIDN'T HOMER* (1,060). He's seventh in career WAR (142.6), and had an MLB-best 15 seasons with at least 300 total bases—more than Eddie Mathews (6), Mickey Mantle (5), and Tony Gwynn (3) *combined.*

Three Aces

It's a pretty good hand in poker, and, as it turns out, it's unbeatable in the National League East.

The Hall of Fame pitching trio of Tom Glavine, John Smoltz, and Greg Maddux played together for ten seasons, from 1993–2002, helping the Braves win every division crown during that span. They are credited most for Atlanta's success at the time, but, let's not forget Chipper Jones.

Jones, a career Brave (1993–2012; .303 BA, 468 HRs), was one of the best third basemen in history, and the only one at the hot corner with at least 2,500 hits and 1,500 walks. His .930 OPS, .529 slugging

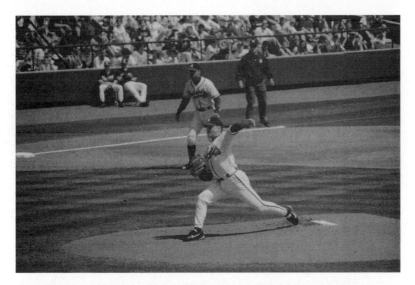

Tom Glavine, pitching in spring training prior to his 1998 Cy Young season. Future Hall of Fame third baseman Chipper Jones in the background. (2 on a Whim Creations, CC BY 2.0)

percentage, and 1,623 RBIs are all tops among primary third basemen. His .470 on-base percentage in 2008 is a Braves record, regardless of position—no one in baseball has matched it since.

In addition to Jones, All-Stars like Fred McGriff (1993–97; 34 HRs/162 avg) and David Justice (1989–96; 32 HRs/162 avg) were actually quite formidable at the plate for Atlanta. . . . But why bury the lead? That era for Braves baseball was all about the bump.

Tom Glavine *(1987–2002, '08; 244 Ws, 3.41 ERA)*: It's a tired analogy, but, like Scottie Pippen to Michael Jordan, Tom Glavine, though great, played very much in the shadow of the incomparable Greg Maddux. But, it still doesn't diminish the fact that Glavine was among the game's best lefties of his generation.

Glavine led all qualified left-handed National League pitchers in ERA in the 1990s (3.21). Sure, Maddux, a right-hander, bested him with a 2.54, but they were still the only two NL pitchers that decade with ERAs below 3.30 (minimum 200 games).

And he was one of the best two-way players of his era, hitting .245 over a four-year stretch, from 1995–98, while his opponents batted just .240 against him.

Glavine knew how to turn it up when necessary—in 1997, opponents batted .239 against him with the bases empty. That number shrunk to .204 with men on base, and then just .184 with runners in scoring position.

John Smoltz *(1988–2008; 210 Ws, 154 SVs, 3.26 ERA)*: Like his placement in this chapter, Smoltz, in both style and substance, fell somewhere in between Glavine and Maddux.

He was a power pitcher, twice leading the league in strikeouts, and still holding the career postseason strikeout record (199). But, midway through his career, he developed impeccable control, topping Glavine's best ever strikeout-to-walk ratio (2.78) each of his final seven full seasons as a starter.

Smoltz underwent Tommy John elbow ligament surgery prior to the 2000 season, and, as a result, found himself relegated to bullpen work for a while—where he thrived. He led the league in saves his first full season as the Braves closer in 2002 (55 SVs) and ended up the all-time saves leader among pitchers with at least 200 wins (154 SVs). Smoltz is also the all-time Tommy John surgery strikeout leader, with 3,084 Ks. Tommy John himself is fourth, with 2,245.

Greg Maddux *(1993–2003; 194 Ws, 2.63 ERA)*: Maddux made 363 career starts for the Braves and never once had consecutive starts in which he failed to throw at least five innings. He had an MLB-record 244 career starts without surrendering a single walk. In short—he was in control.

During a completely dominant stretch in which he won four-consecutive Cy Youngs (1992–95), Maddux averaged a 1.98 ERA, a 202 ERA+, and a 0.953 WHIP. Only six other pitchers in the last 100 years have even recorded a *single* season with a 201 or better ERA+ and a WHIP of 0.953 or less. Amazingly, two of those occurred in 2015—Zack Greinke with a 225 ERA+ and 0.844 WHIP and Jake Arrieta with a 222 ERA+ and 0.865 WHIP.

Maddux is the only pitcher in league history with a 260 ERA+ season—and he did it TWICE, *in consecutive seasons,* from 1994–95 (271, 260, respectively). All-Century Team member Nolan Ryan had a career-best 195 ERA+ in 1981, while Maddux averaged a 195 ERA+ over six seasons, from 1993–98. He's tied with Curt Schilling for the most seasons with a 6.00+ strikeout-to-walk ratio (4), and he's the only pitcher in league history to notch 180+ strikeouts with less than 25 walks in the same season (181 Ks, 23 BBs; 1995).

[Balls & Strikes- Maddux walked just 121 batters on four pitches during his eleven seasons with the Braves; 63.6% (77) of them were intentional walks. He averaged 1.65 strikeouts per BALL THREE during his Braves career, and during a stretch from July 16, 1993 to May 13, 2000, he issued just 212 bases on balls in 213 total starts.]

Atlanta also frequently surrounded their trio of aces with capable arms to help carry the load. The 1998 Braves are the only team in baseball history with five 150+ strikeout pitchers (Maddux, 204; Smoltz, 173; Denny Neagle, 165; Kevin Millwood, 163; Glavine, 157).

STATS INCREDIBLE!

3: The amount of players that struck out five times in a single game last season. Hank Aaron never once in his 23-year career ever struck out more than three times in a game.

37: Greg Maddux won four straight Cy Young Awards from 1992–95. He had 37 CGs to just 33 HRs allowed during that span.

.248: The Braves' win percentage in 1935 (38–115)—the second-worst finish since 1900. Incidentally, also Babe Ruth's last team in the big leagues.

10: Major-league record number of seasons in which Maddux stole at least one base without being caught.

30/30: In 1991, Braves outfielder Ron Gant became just the fourth player in MLB history with multiple 30+ home run/30+ stolen base seasons (Willie Mays, Bobby Bonds, Howard Johnson).

.198: Melvin Upton Jr.'s batting average during his Braves career (267 games). Pitcher Tom Glavine batted .226 for the Braves from 1991–98 (267 games).

266: Complete games pitched by Warren Spahn in which he allowed two or fewer runs. No other pitcher during the Live Ball Era (post-1919) even has 200.

107: Career games in which Greg Maddux pitched 7+ innings, surrendered two or fewer runs, and did not win—a Live Ball record.

294: Phil Niekro's record for games started after turning forty.

237: Hugh Duffy's former single-season hits record (now T-21st) for the Beaneaters in 1894, after playing in just 125 games. His 162-game pace would have netted him 307 hits. It's the second-highest hits total for a player under five-foot-eight.

58: Total pitches thrown by Red Barrett in a nine-inning complete-game shutout on August 10, 1944. It's the lowest pitch total for a CG SHO in MLB history.

25/25: Center fielder Andruw Jones, winner of ten straight Gold Gloves (1998–2007), had 25+ home runs and 25+ defensive runs saved in four straight seasons, from 1998–2001. No other outfielder in history has more than one such 25+/25+ season.

19: Andruw Jones's age in 1996, making him the youngest player to homer in a postseason game (Game 7, NLCS; 19 years, 177 days), and youngest player to homer in a World Series game (Game 1; 19 years, 180 days).

174: From May 1, 1942 to June 22, 1947, pitcher Johnny Sain had 174 straight plate appearances, as a batter, without a strikeout.

2.21: Jonny Sain returned to baseball in 1946 after serving three years in the United States Navy. He had a 2.21 ERA and no strikeouts in 104 plate appearances at bat.

1.60: ERA of Greg Maddux from 1994 to 1995. The last qualified pitcher with an ERA that low in a *single* season was . . . Greg Maddux.

47: Hank Aaron's career-high home run total in 1971, at age thirty-seven. He played in just 139 games that season.

42.8: Pitcher Johnny Sain had just 20 strikeouts in 856 plate appearances, averaging 42.8 plate appearances per strikeout. By comparison, Tony Gwynn averaged a strikeout per every 23.6 plate appearances during his career.

MIAMI MARLINS

Est. 1993

Coming into the 2016 season, Jose Fernandez will be twenty-three years old with 47 career starts and a sparkling 2.40 ERA. The last pitcher with at least as many starts and a better ERA through age twenty-three was Babe Ruth.

As a franchise, the Marlins are not too dissimilar to the Philadelphia Athletics. Both teams had success in between periods of complete futility. Surely, the Marlins wouldn't mind matching the A's championship tally in Philly (5), but they'd probably prefer to keep their operation on the east coast.

Miami, then known as the *Florida* Marlins, was an expansion franchise in 1993. To their credit, they were the fastest expansion team in history, at the time, to win the World Series (1997), and are still the fastest expansion team to two championships (2003). The Marlins, however, have never won a division, have only qualified for the postseason twice, have, at times, alienated the fan base with controversial roster overhauls, and have finished either last or second-to-last in NL attendance for 15 of the last 17 years. If all this adversity seems like a mountain overlooking a mole hill of positives, consider—the Phillies waited 97 years to get their first championship . . . and another 28 years to get their second.

Obviously, World Series rings are important. The Marlins have two while the Rays, Rangers, Brewers, Astros, Padres, Mariners, Rockies, and Nationals are all still seeking their first. It's hard not to consider the team a success. And there has always seemed to be a method to their madness.

Miami has been a master at building contenders from the ground up. Three key homegrown players—Charles Johnson (C), Edgar Renteria (SS), and Luis Castillo (2B)—all got their start in baseball with the Marlins in 1992. Renteria had the game-winning hit in the 1997 World Series over the Cleveland Indians, and Hernandez would take home the Series MVP. Castillo, while not much of a factor that season, played more games in a Marlins uniform than any other player (1,128), and is in the top 10 in most franchise offensive categories. The team has built around young, core players like this at several turns in its history.

Miguel Cabrera (2003), Hanley Ramirez (2006), and Giancarlo Stanton (2010) all spent their rookie seasons with the Marlins, and are three of the best baseball products of the twenty-first century. But, the team's best never seem to stick around.

As the Marlins build, the trend seems to be that they trade their best veteran talent for young players . . . that eventually become their best veteran talent that is baited down the line for new, fresh fish. It's a volatile business model, and regardless of how the team's successes and failures are measured, Miami's biggest challenge may be resisting the temptation to sell off, not just their best players, but their franchise in its entirety.

1997

Renteria and Hernandez were the young World Series heroes, but the championship club in 1997 consisted of mostly thirty-plus-year-old veteran talent.

Kevin Brown (SP, age thirty-two), Moises Alou (OF, thirty), Gary Sheffield (OF, twenty-eight), and Bobby Bonilla (3B, thirty-four) all finished in the top five in WAR for the team that season, playing significant roles. By the end of the following season, all four would be just a memory with the Marlins. But a good one.

Brown had the best two-year stretch of his career with the Marlins in 1996–97, going 33–19 overall with a 2.30 ERA. Brown only spent those two seasons with the Fish, but still ranks third in total pitching WAR in team history (15). He was *that* good.

Leading the league with a 1.89 ERA in 1996, Brown became one of just 11 National League players in 30 years (1967–96) to record an ERA below 2.00. He was effective, though sometimes erratic, hitting a league-leading 16 batters that year. No other NL player in history, with an ERA that low, hit as many batters as Brown.

Nineteen ninety-six was also a special year for Sheffield. The 500–home run club member had a career-high 1.090 OPS that season, batting .314/.465/.624. Sheff (142 BBs) and Barry Bonds (151 BBs) became the first NL players since Jim Wynn in 1969 (and fourth and fifth NL players overall) to have a 140+ walk season. Sheffield is one of just four players in league history (with Bonds, Jeff Bagwell, and Mark McGwire) with a 40+ home run, 120+ RBI, 140+ walk season.

The Marlins had a lot of star power on that 1997 squad, but, in terms of WAR, their best position player was catcher Charles Johnson (4.4)—a defensive prodigy, operating in anonymity. The four-time Gold Glove winner had the highest defensive WAR in the league in 1997 (2.6)—the year he allowed just one passed ball while never committing a single error. He didn't see any significant playing time until 1995, but Johnson still ranks third in the league in total defensive WAR during the 1990s (9.6).

2003

What a story.

The Marlins were 15–21 to start 2003. From there, they hired a new coach (Jack McKeon), called up a couple young studs (Dontrelle Willis and Miguel Cabrera) and, you know, went on to win the World Series. Ho-hum.

The Marlins were in last place in the division as late as June 18th (34–39), but went 58–32 the rest of the way, to capture the NL Wild Card and make their second improbable run for glory.

Small-ball was a key component of the '03 team. They had the best 1-2 hole hitters in baseball, with Juan Pierre (204 hits and 65 stolen bases) and Luis Castillo (187 Hs, 21 SBs) leading things off. No other 1-2 combination in the game had as many hits or stolen bases that year.

Dontrelle Willis caught the league by storm that year, going 14–6 with a 3.30 ERA, and one of the wackiest deliveries in baseball history.

Willis's pitching motion was a combination of Nolan Ryan's high-leg kick and Nuke Laloosh's skyward mid-delivery stare. It worked great for a time, as Willis won the franchise's first Rookie of the Year award at season's end, and finished runner-up for the Cy Young two years later. Though he lost his magic touch prematurely, pitching his final full season by 2007, Willis still made an indelible mark on the franchise.

After his final year with Miami, Willis was the franchise leader in pitching WAR (17.1), and is currently second behind Josh Johnson (25.4). Over a three-year stretch, from 2003–05, Willis (46–27, 3.27 ERA) was one of only three pitchers in the National League with at least 45 wins and a sub-4.00 ERA.

Miguel Cabrera, finishing fifth for Rookie of the Year in '03, had a hot start and kept on going. With an eight-year (and counting) career in Detroit that has seen Miggy win a Triple Crown, two

MVPs, and four of the past five AL batting titles, it may be easy to forget how great he was with Miami.

Batting .339 with 26 home runs in 2006, Cabrera became the first, and only, third baseman in NL history to bat .338+ with 25+ home runs. You don't have to look much further than how the Marlins performed with Miggy on the field versus when he was off it. They were 35–40 (.467) without him in 2003, but 56–31 (.644) with him. He led them to a 11–6 (.647) record in the postseason en route to capturing their second World Series crown.

In Marlins history, no position player, over any qualifying amount of plate appearances, has touched Cabrera's .313/.388/.542 slash line with the team, and he currently ranks first in team history batting average, second in OPS (.929), and fourth in total WAR (18.2).

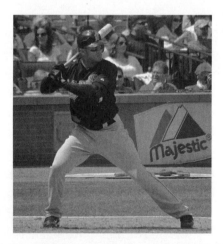

Giancarlo Stanton in 2011, just the fourth player in MLB history to club 34 home runs in his age-twenty-one season. (Flickr d-dee, CC BY 2.0)

The Future

Dee Gordon and Giancarlo Stanton are two of the young, core players Miami hopes to build around. The newbie Gordon arrived in Miami during the 2014 offseason, and had a memorable Marlins debut in 2015.

A .272 career hitter in four seasons prior to landing in South Beach, Gordon came out of nowhere to win a batting title in 2015, hitting .333. He also led the NL in stolen bases (58), becoming the first player since Jackie Robinson in 1949 to lead the National League in both categories. His 11 multi-hit, multi-steal games were the most in baseball since Tony Womack had 11 in 1997. Gordon's the first infielder ever to win a batting title, stolen base crown, and Gold Glove in the same season, and the second player to do so at any position (Ichiro Suzuki, 2001).

Stanton, the tallest position player in team history, at six-foot-six, hit 154 home runs before his age-twenty-five season. Only six other players in league history have ever done that, and they're all in the Hall of Fame. His 181 home runs this decade are the most in the National League, and he's probably just scratching the surface of his potential.

He finished 10th in the league in home runs, with 27 in 2015, after playing in only 74 games. Both he and Albert Pujols had 181 homers through 708 career games. That's 39 more homers, through Stanton's first six seasons, than his new hitting coach and all-time home run king, Barry Bonds, had through his first six seasons—despite the fact that Bonds played exactly one full season worth of games more—870 to 708.

2016 might be a special season for Stanton and the Fish.

STATS INCREDIBLE!

8: Total amount of triples for catcher Mike Piazza, throughout a 16-year MLB career. He had at least one with each of the five teams he played for though, including the Marlins, with whom he played just five games in 1998.

130: Juan Pierre's career plate appearances with the bases loaded. He batted .381/.408/.487 and struck out just twice.

8: 2013 Rookie of the Year Jose Fernandez became just the fourth pitcher in history with 8+ strikeouts in at least half of his first 34 career games.

2.19: Fernandez's ERA was the lowest for a first-year pitcher since 1913 (Reb Russell, 1.90).

94.5: Mat Latos's ERA after his first start of 2015, AND *Southwest Florida's Classic Rock Station.*

188: Career stolen bases of Dee Gordon, through five seasons—more than his father, Tom Gordon, allowed during his 21-year career (167).

0.4: Juan Pierre's WAR in 2005, playing in all 162 games. Barry Bonds had a 0.6, playing in just 14 games.

9.02%: 200 of Pierre's 2,217 (or 9.02%) career hits were bunt-hits.

41: Times Pierre faced Hall of Famer Greg Maddux in his career. He batted .342 and never struck out. Only Tony Gwynn faced Maddux more times without a K. He faced *future* Hall of Famer Curt Schilling 40 times, batting .385 and striking out just once.

5,136: Days between Suzuki's first home runs for both the Mariners (2001) and Marlins (2015). He's the first Japanese-born player to homer for each franchise.

708: Games played by Stanton through 2015, clubbing 181 home runs—the same number that Albert Pujols had through 708 career games.

25: Stanton's cumulative WAR from age twenty to twenty-five, with 181 home runs in 708 games. Miguel Cabrera, from age twenty to twenty-five, had 4.1 fewer WAR, and six fewer home runs, despite 172 *more* games played.

NEW YORK METS

Est. 1962

Michael Conforto is the only player in baseball history with an RBI in the Little League World Series, College World Series, and MLB World Series.

The New York Mets, founded in 1962, are not one of baseball's oldest franchises—not even close. In their relatively brief existence, however, they have proven to be one of its most popular, and compelling teams.

Sure, that's easy to say after a World Series berth in 2015, when teen idol Jacob deGrom blew away the competition, flowing locks draped below his cap like a superhero cape. But, the Mets have seamlessly melded into national pastime lore, through both good times and bad.

Their first four seasons were historically dreadful, debuting with the third-worst record in modern baseball history in 1962 (40–120) and playing just .300 ball through 1965 (194–452). Naturally, they were dubbed the "Miracle Mets" after a 100-win, World Series championship season in 1969, considering the team had never previously eclipsed 73 wins in a single season.

[Did you know?: The Mets' color scheme is a combination of the Brooklyn Dodgers' blue, and the New York Giants' orange—both

teams that split the Big Apple for the West Coast, opening up a spot for the expansion Metropolitans.]

Ace Tom Seaver played a big role in the turnaround. He won the Rookie of the Year in 1967, and the Cy Young in 1969, going 25–7, accounting for 25% of his team's wins and just 11% of its losses. History may not grant Seaver proper credit, but he was as singularly responsible for the Mets' amazing turnaround as was any one player for any one team, ever.

Adding Seaver paid big dividends for New York, even though, during the phenom's first ten big league seasons, the team finished just a shade under .500 (804–809; .498). In the 1980s, the Mets doubled up, drafting *two* wunderkinds, setting up the longest sustained stretch of contention in franchise history.

Outfielder Darryl Strawberry and ace righty Dwight Gooden are remembered as the faces of the Mets in the 1980s, but their 1986 club was historically well-balanced, winning the franchise's second World Series after a 108-win regular season—the fourth-highest win total in National League history. The team had everything:

- ✔ *Power-hitting superstar (Strawberry)*
- ✔ *Unhittable ace (Gooden)*
- ✔ *Unhittable backup aces (Ron Darling, Bob Ojeda)*
- ✔ *Hall of Fame catcher (Gary Carter)*
- ✔ *Sweet-swinging mustachioed first baseman (Keith Hernandez)*
- ✔ *Prototype leadoff man (Lenny Dykstra)*

The Mets averaged an impressive 95 wins per season from Gooden's rookie year (1984) until 1990. That's an amazing run, for sure, but the team seemed capable of more.

By 1991, not a single starting position player remained from the '86 club. By 1993, they finished with their worst record since

Doc Gooden warming up at Candlestick Park in 1991. (Brad Hunter)

1966 (59–103; .364). They rebounded at the turn of the century, reaching the World Series in 2000, but, in total, the Mets have only reached the postseason four times since 1988. It's been a struggle regaining that magic from 30 years ago.

Until now?

Finally, all the pieces seem to be in place for New York's Mets. DeGrom, the 2014 Rookie of the Year, leads an exciting, young, and deeply talented club that could be a problem for the rest of the National League for a very long time. It's a wonderful resurgence that is absolutely amazin', but not the least bit surprisin'.

Summer of '69

If you were to look back at a 1969 Mets lineup card, it might be difficult to pin 100 wins on them and a World Series title. They finished below the league average in every discernible offensive category—you'd have to invent a new stat, like EAR (Effort Above Replacement) to shine a positive light on their offensive output. The nine players on the team with at least 300 at-bats combined for just five All-Star appearances for their entire careers. Current Mets third baseman David Wright has seven so far, all by himself. The Mets' pitching staff had to be stellar, and it was.

They finished second in the league in ERA in 1969 (2.99) and first in WHIP (1.181). Starters Tom Seaver and Jerry Koosman carried the load.

Koosman was phenomenal that year (17–9, 2.28 ERA), but Seaver finished with the Cy Young, at 25–7 with a 2.21 ERA. Only two other pitchers (Steve Carlton and Ron Guidry) have recorded a season with 25+ wins and a sub-2.25 ERA since. And it may not have been his best statistical season.

Seaver won three ERA titles during his first seven years in baseball (1970–71, 1973; 1967–73) maintaining a 2.38 overall—the lowest ERA in the game during that span. Hall of Famer Randy Johnson never pitched a single season with an ERA of 2.25 or better, but Seaver averaged a 2.25 mark over a *four-season stretch*, from 1968–71.

He was probably the '70s' best, earning top marks in the National League during the decade in ERA (2.61) and wins (tied–178; Carlton). Hall of Famer Tom Glavine's best single-season WHIP was a 1.095 in 1991—Seaver maintained 1.073 for the *entire decade*.

The Great '80s

The Dodgers won one more title than the Mets during the 1980s (2 to 1), but New York probably had the most talent all the way through. They were stacked.

Darryl Strawberry *(OF, 1983–90)*: The Mets' all-time home run leader (252) took Rookie of the Year honors in his debut season, and was a force throughout his Mets career, averaging 32 home runs per season. He never clubbed fewer than 26 home runs with New York and was the first player in baseball history with 15+ home runs and 15+ stolen bases in each of his first six seasons. The only player to do it since? Barry Bonds.

He's one of only seven NL players with 300+ home runs before age thirty (342). After age thirty, Strawberry hit just 55 home runs over his final eight seasons.

Dwight Gooden *(SP, 1984–94)*: Doc followed up his 1984 Rookie of the Year campaign by winning pitching's Triple Crown in 1985 (NL-leading 24 Ws, 1.53 ERA, 268 Ks). At just twenty years old, he became the youngest to take the Crown, and the youngest Cy Young winner in history. Gooden certainly peaked early, recording the highest single-season strikeout total for a teenager in 1984 (276; age nineteen), and the lowest ERA in a sophomore season (1.53) since Dutch Leonard's Deadball Era 0.96 in 1914.

Gooden never had an ERA above 3.83 during his nine full seasons with the Mets, but, like Strawberry, his career is lopsided, marred by unfulfilled potential. His 157-win total before age thirty is the best in baseball since Catfish Hunter's 1975 season (184 Ws). He would win just 37 games in five seasons then after.

Keith Hernandez *(1B, 1984–88)* and **Gary Carter** *(C, 1985–89)*: Hernandez and Carter were two very accomplished players before joining the Mets, and lucky for New York, they enjoyed some of their best seasons *after* age thirty.

Hernandez wasn't a big home run hitter with the Mets (80 dingers in seven seasons), but he was the franchise's most complete player at the position. He leads all Mets first basemen in batting average (.297; minimum 500 games), and won twice as many Gold Gloves as any other Met (5; 1984–89).

Carter hit 100+ RBIs his first two seasons with New York. His three 100+ RBI seasons after his thirtieth birthday are the most among thirty-plus-year-old catchers in baseball history. Sure, former Mets backstop Mike Piazza did it six times, but Carter is still one of just eight catchers in league history to bat .280+ with 30+ home runs and 100+ RBIs in a single season (.281, 32 HRs, 100 RBIs; 1985).

2015 and Beyond

The 2015 Mets took the division and the NLCS in much of the same way the 1969 club did it—with great pitching.

Sophomore ace Jacob deGrom already has twice as many sub-1.150 WHIP seasons as Hall of Famer Bob Feller. No wonder this Mets tale sounds familiar: deGrom is one of just five pitchers since 1968 to pitch a sub-1.000 WHIP season by his sophomore year, joining Mets brothers in arms Tom Seaver, Doc Gooden, and Matt Harvey (Marlins pitcher Jose Fernandez is the fifth).

Before deGrom, Harvey was the new instant-ace to join Mets lore. He was dominant in his 2013 rookie year, posting the third-best ERA in the league (2.27), and an MLB-best 2.01 FIP. Actually, Harvey and Gooden (1.89) are the only rookies in league history with an FIP that low.

Harvey then sat out 2014 after Tommy John surgery, and the baseball gods (seemingly) awarded the Mets deGrom. Only fair . . . except for the embarrassment of pitching riches that collided once Harvey returned. The right-hander rebounded with the sixth best ERA in the league in 2015 (2.77), joining deGrom (2.54) for one of the best one-two punches in the game. Unlike the '69 Amazins, these pitchers had help from the offense.

The Mets finished third-to-last in the league in batting average (.244), but were also third in home runs (177) and fourth in OPS+

Jacob deGrom (foreground), taking the field against the Baltimore Orioles in 2015. Jacob deGrom's hair (background) follows close behind. (Keith Allison; KeithAllisonPhoto.com)

(98). Deadline deal addition Yoenis Cespedes was as valuable down the stretch as anyone on the roster, clubbing 17 home runs in 249 Mets plate appearances—the third-most in the NL since he switched leagues. His 2.3 WAR, on paper, wouldn't have made a difference either way in the Mets' division win, with seven games to spare. The added aspect of collective danger he brought to New York's lineup, however, is incalculable.

STATS INCREDIBLE!

9: Matt Harvey's win total in 2013. The first sub-2.50 ERA pitcher in history with 175+ innings pitched and 175+ strikeouts to not reach double-digit wins.

20/20: The 1988 Mets were the first team in baseball history to have three players with 20 home runs and 20 stolen bases (Darryl Strawberry, Kevin McReynolds, Howard Johnson).

.390: Dave Magadan's on-base percentage during his 16-year career (1986–2001). It's the highest OBP for a non-All-Star infielder since the All-Star Game was started in 1933.

.534: Mike Piazza's career slugging percentage against fellow Hall of Famers (including postseason), with 20 home runs, in 307 plate appearances. The only Hall of Fame pitcher he faced without homering was Dennis Eckersley—though he batted .600 against him. He also batted .364/.440/.955 in 25 career plate appearances against Roger Clemens, with four home runs.

411: Tom Seaver's MLB record for consecutive starts with at least one strikeout.

3: World Series record for blown saves, "accomplished" by closer Jeurys Familia in 2015.

42: Bartolo Colon's age during the 2015 offseason, becoming the oldest player to pitch in extra innings of a World Series game since Dolf Luque (age forty-four) in 1933.

6: Consecutive postseason games in which second baseman Daniel Murphy homered, an MLB record. No Met has even homered in six straight *regular* season games.

40: Rickey Henderson had seven stolen bases in ten postseason games in 1999. He had three steals just in Game 2 of the 1999 NLDS. He was forty years old.

7.6: John Olerud had a 7.6 WAR in 1998, besting both Mark McGwire (7.5) and Sammy Sosa (6.4) as they chased Roger Maris.

15: Mike Piazza had an RBI in 15 straight games from June 14 to July 2, 2000—the longest streak since Ray Grimes had a record 17 straight in 1922.

3: Curtis Granderson became the first player with three go-ahead home runs in a World Series for the losing team since Babe Ruth in 1926.

[Babe Ruth was caught stealing in the ninth inning with two outs and the Yankees down a run with Bob Meusel at bat and Lou Gehrig on deck in Game 7 to lose that World Series for the Yankees.]

19: Strikeouts by Tom Seaver in a single game on April 22, 1970 (an MLB record at the time). He pitched a 2-hit complete game over the Padres, and struck out the last 10 batters he faced, still a major league record.

449: Matt Harvey's strikeout total, against just 94 walks, in 65 career games. No pitcher in history has more Ks with fewer BBs through their first 65 games.

1,251: Amount of pitches rookie starter Noah Syndergaard has thrown at 96+ MPH in his short career (of 2,380 pitches total). Three-time Cy Young winner Clayton Kershaw has thrown 1,114 career pitches at 95+ MPH.

3: Go-ahead home runs by Curtis Granderson in the 2015 World Series. Derek Jeter had just two in his long postseason career. Granderson is the first leadoff man with multiple go-ahead homers in one Series.

PHILADELPHIA PHILLIES

Est. 1883

On May 29, 2010, Roy Halladay tossed the 20th perfect game in MLB history. Just 130 days later, on October 6, 2010, he no-hit the Reds in Game 1 of the NLDS. He is just one of six pitchers to throw two no-hitters in one season and the only *pitcher to throw a no-hitter in both the regular season and postseason.*

The Phillies last won a World Series in 2008—100 years more recently than the Chicago Cubs (1908). Yet, the Cubs are baseball's notorious, cuddly, lovable losers, while, historically, the Phillies have been, well . . . less cuddly and lovable.

In 2007, Philadelphia was the first pro franchise to reach 10,000 losses, and to this day, it ranks atop the all-time list (10,650). In terms of winning percentage, it's the worst franchise established prior to 1969 (.472), and the only nineteenth century-born team under .500.

It hasn't always been sunny in Philadelphia. But, like the Cubs (and maybe more so), there is a lot to love about this team.

While things started off dreadfully for Philly (17–81; 1883), the club actually played well overall in its 20 seasons prior to the World Series era (1903–present), finishing over .500 13 times from 1883–1902. Things took a turn for the Phils at the start of the twentieth century, but they're not entirely to blame for their own misfortune.

The Athletics set up shop in Philadelphia as part of American League expansion of Major League Baseball in 1901, and things got hostile in the City of Brotherly Love. Connie Mack, shrewd owner and manager of the upstart A's, poached the Phils' roster, most notably stealing away Nap Lajoie, one of the greatest batsmen in the game's history.

Lajoie batted .426 that year with the A's, establishing the single-season modern era record, and royally pissing off the Phillies. In a desperate attempt to win back the star second baseman, the Phils had Lajoie's crosstown jump deemed illegal, and, starting in 1902, the only Pennsylvania team that could justly claim him was the Phillies.

Naturally, Mack then traded his rights to Cleveland, where Lajoie played so well, they named the team after him. Fortune did not favor the Phillies for quite some time then after.

The Phils made an unsuccessful World Series run in 1915, but, over a 31-year stretch from 1918–48, the Phillies had just one winning season. 31 *years*!

No wonder Phillies fans are so fond of their near-misses— especially the NL Champion "Whiz Kids" in 1950 and the "Macho Row" club in 1993—because actual championship glory was so rare. Moreover, on September 20, 1964, with just a dozen games remaining in the season, the Phillies had a commanding 6.5-game lead in the National League, all but assuring a trip to World Series. However, as Yogi Berra once said, "It ain't over till it's over," and Gene Mauch's Phillies would prove that—dropping ten of the final twelve games, surrendering the National League title to the would-be World Champion Cardinals. But after a 97-year drought, the Phillies won their first championship in 1980, and then, after a 20-year all-sports city-wide drought, they won their second in 2008.

Baker Bowl (1920), baseball's first "bandbox," featured a right field wall just 280 feet from home plate, but roughly 24 feet higher than Boston's Green Monster. (Anonymous)

Citizens Bank Park, 2007. High walls and an inward-angled left-center-field wall are prominent features of each. While Baker Bowl's right field fence stood 60 feet high, CBP's is a comparatively-short 13.3 feet. (en. Wikipedia Phillyfan0419, PD)

Any other team, in any other city, might not have survived the lulls that so often plagued Philadelphia's Phillies. But, the City of Brotherly Love—and often Love-Hate—has always had its arms firmly wrapped around its hometown Fightin' Phils.

Old Pete & Chucky

The Phillies' pennant-winning 1915 club owes a lot of its success to **Grover Cleveland Alexander** *(SP, 1911–17)*, one of the team's, and league's, all-time best pitchers. Dead ball or not, Old Pete dominated that season, winning his first of three pitching Triple Crowns (31 Ws, 1.22 ERA, 241 Ks) and accounting for 34% of Philadelphia's total wins on the year (90).

That year, Alexander was the first NL pitcher with 195+ strikeouts, a 195+ ERA+, and sub-1.95 FIP, and only two pitchers in league history have since joined the club—Bob Gibson (1968) and Clayton Kershaw (2014).

Nineteen fifteen was just the beginning for Alexander, though. In 1916, he won his second consecutive Triple Crown (33 Ws, 1.55 ERA, 167 Ks), setting a new franchise record for wins in a single season that still stands. Nineteen seventeen was his third straight season with 30+ wins (30 Ws, 1.83 ERA, 200 Ks), but it would be his last in Philadelphia.

The Phillies reportedly dealt him in anticipation of the thirty-year old being drafted in World War I, and were correct in their assumption. Alexander returned from combat a changed man—he won another Triple Crown with Chicago in 1920, but injuries, illness, and alcoholism stymied his potential and quality of life.

Chuck Klein *(OF, 1928–33, 1936–44)* didn't exactly reign over a successful term in Phillies history, but he was the club's best player (and league MVP) during that aforementioned single winning season (1932) in more than three decades (1918–48). He was one of the game's greatest talents, on one of its poorest teams.

Klein was, at the time, the fastest player to reach 100 career home runs (390 games) and is still the fastest to 1,000 career hits (683 games).

He's the only player in baseball history with a season of 50+ doubles, 10+ triples, 30+ home runs, and 20+ steals (1932). That season also made Klein the first player in history with multiple 50+ 2B/30+ HR seasons (1930, 1932)—a feat unmatched for nearly 70 years, before Todd Helton (2000–01) and Albert Pujols (2003–04, 2012) finally joined the club.

Klein and Rogers Hornsby are the only members of baseball's 40/140 club (home runs/singles). No other player has joined their ranks since Klein slugged 40 homers with 143 singles in 1930.

The shallow right field wall at Klein's home field Baker Bowl is credited for boosting his offensive performance, but it often allowed outfielders to play in and turn would-be singles into outs. To be fair, Klein, as a right fielder, also turned this to his advantage,

This diagram illustrates the main differences in size between Baker Bowl and Citizens Bank Park. Notice the short distance to Baker Bowl's right field fence. Sixty feet high, the wall was 62% higher than Boston's famed "Green Monster." (Brian Dainis, Curotec)

recording 44 outfield assists in 1930—yet another MLB record that still stands.

Schmitty and Lefty

Mike "Schmitty" Schmidt *(3B, 1972–89)* and Steve "Lefty" Carlton *(SP, 1972–86)* were two of the best players of their generation, and are most commonly described as the two best players in team history. It's no surprise, then, that the Phillies were finally able to win their first World Series, after 78 years trying, while their two best players dominated the competition.

Schmidt (.286 BA, 48 HRs, 121 RBIs) and Carlton (24 Ws, 2.34 ERA, 286 Ks) won the National League MVP and Cy Young award, respectively, carrying the Phils to 91 regular season wins, an NL East division crown, and eventual World Series victory over the Kansas City Royals in 1980. It was a tremendous team victory—the only franchise championship until 2008—but both players were among Philadelphia's most consistent and dominant individual champions.

Schmitty is the franchise's best player, all-time. His total Phillies career WAR alone (106.5) is just a win shy of Jimmy Rollins and Chase Utley . . . combined. He also leads the team in defensive WAR (17.6), Gold Gloves (10), home runs (548), RBIs (1,595), runs scored (1,506), total bases (4,404), walks (1,507), extra-base hits (1,015), times on base (3,820), and times mentioned as the game's greatest third baseman (a gazillion).

He's the only player in history to amass 500 home runs from the hot corner (509). No one hit more out in the 1980s (313), and only the Babe led the league in homers more times than Schmitty (11 to 6). With all that power, it's sometimes forgotten that the converted shortstop was also fleet of foot.

Schmidt had as many seasons with 35+ home runs and at least a dozen stolen bases (6) as Barry Bonds had.

*Mike Schmidt at Philadelphia's Veterans Stadium, hitting a home run
off the Reds—his 21st home run of the season and 516th of his career.*
(Squelle, CC BY-SA 3.0)

On the pitching side, **Lefty** was every bit as dominant for
the Phillies as Schmidt. The 329-game winner (a franchise-best
241 with Philadelphia) retired with a then-record four Cy Young
Awards, all with Philadelphia. In the 11 seasons that spanned his
first Cy Young season to his last (1972–82), Carlton averaged 19
wins and 226 strikeouts, with a 2.96 ERA.

In 1972, his first season with the team, Lefty won the NL Triple
Crown (27 Ws, 1.97 ERA, 310 Ks) and accounted for 45.8% of the
team's victories (59). He had six complete games, with a 3.79 ERA
in his 10 losses.

His 10 losses that season were made possible by the Phillies'
futile offense, which scored no more than one run in five of them
and no more than two runs in seven. His 27 wins were almost
impossible. Since 1953, only Denny McLain (31 Ws; 1968) has
won more games in a single season—and Lefty won his with the

"support" of the second-worst offensive team in the National League (3.22 runs per game). Carlton and Sandy Koufax are the only pitchers of the Live Ball Era (post-1920) with a 25+ win/ sub-2.00 ERA/ 300+ strikeout season.

Unfortunately for the Phillies, the rest of the team went just 32–87 in 1972, with a collective 4.22 ERA.

In stark contrast, Philadelphia's 2011 rotation was stacked, top to bottom.

The Core Four

The Phillies entered the twenty-first century having finished over .500 just once in the previous 16 seasons. As a franchise, they turned their focus toward building up a long-neglected farm system through the MLB draft, and the results were a great success. Home grown products Jimmy Rollins, Chase Utley, Ryan Howard, and Cole Hamels were the franchise cornerstones for a decade, and some of the greatest talents to ever wear the uniform.

Rollins *(SS, 2000–14)* was arguably the greatest shortstop in team history. He's the franchise leader in hits (2,306), doubles (479), and second in extra-base hits (806). He accomplished a lot in his 15 years with Philadelphia, but one season sticks out in particular.

In 2007, Rollins won league MVP honors, totaling 20 triples, 30 home runs, and 41 stolen bases. He's the only player in history with a 20/30/40 season. Rollins is the only Phillie since Nap Lajoie in 1897 to have a 20-triple year, and he's one of just seven MLB players ever with 20+ triples and 20+ home runs in the same season—the first NL player to pull the feat since George Brett in 1979.

In his career (through 2015), Rollins has totaled 114 triples, 229 homers, and 465 stolen bases. No other single player has ever had more of each. His ten career seasons with 20+ doubles, 10+ home runs, and 30+ stolen bases are also unmatched in MLB history. His four seasons with at least 35 doubles and 35 stolen bases are the most by a shortstop since Honus Wagner had his fifth in 1909.

Part of the best double-play combination in team history, Utley (26) and Rollins (11), together from 2003–14, sealed the bond with a handshake before each game. (Kevin Durso)

Utley *(2B, 2003–15),* in his prime, was one of the best players in baseball, though he never won a league MVP like Howard and Rollins did (2006, 2007, respectively), or a World Series MVP, as did Hamels in 2008. Historically, he should be recognized as one of the most valuable second basemen in team—and baseball—history.

His 62.3 career WAR (thus far) is just 2.8 fewer than Craig Biggio, 4.5 fewer than Roberto Alomar, and 5.2 fewer than Ryne Sandberg—all Hall of Famers. His peak WAR seasons are in very rare company. He had a 17.2 WAR combined in 2008 and 2009, the highest total by a second baseman in consecutive seasons since Hall of Famer Joe Morgan's back-to-back MVP years of 1975 and 1976. From 2005 to 2009, Utley had five straight seasons with at least a 7.0 WAR. Every other second baseman in history with at least four total 7.0 WAR seasons is in the Hall of Fame, including Jackie Robinson (4), Sandberg (4), Charlie Gehringer (5), Morgan (5), Nap Lajoie (7), Eddie Collins (8), and Rogers Hornsby (8).

Utley batted .301/.388/.535 during that five-year peak from 2005 to 2009. Only four other second basemen have slashed that in a *single* season since Robinson broke the color barrier in 1947, and none of them did it twice. Only four other second basemen in history (Biggio, Gehringer, Hornsby, Lajoie) have equaled in a single season the .388 on-base percentage, 73 extra-base hits, and 15 stolen bases Utley averaged over that five-year stretch. Utley's peak also yielded a great deal of World Series success.

He has seven career World Series home runs. Duke Snider is the only National Leaguer with more (11). In 2009, he tied "Mr. October," Reggie Jackson, for most home runs in a single World Series, with five. His career .795 World Series slugging percentage ranks second-best all-time among players with at least 35 plate appearances—edged only by David Ortiz, by six-ten-thousandths of a point.

Howard *(1B, 2004–)* came on strong, reaching 100 career home runs in just 325 games, an MLB record. It was 51 games sooner than runner-up Ralph Kiner. He was also the fastest to 200 (658 games) and the second-fastest to 300 (1,093, six more than Kiner). In 2006, he bested Mike Schmidt's previous single-season franchise home run record by 10, clubbing 58 home runs; in 1945, *the entire Phils team hit 56.* He's the only member of the team's

50+ home run club, and only three other Phillies since the 1920s have even hit 40+ (Schmidt, Jim Thome, Dick Allen).

[From 1871 to 1995, 23 players collected at least five qualified seasons batting .300/.375/.550 or better. Among them are 22 Hall of Famers and Dick Allen.]

From September 6, 2005 to September 9, 2006, "The Big Piece" batted .312/.405/.689 with 65 home runs and 162 RBIs over a 162 game span.

Ryan Howard in 2012, becoming the second-fastest batter to 300 career home runs in baseball history. (Michael Kirk Photography)

Hamels (2006–15) was one of the franchise's greatest starting pitchers, providing Philadelphia with a bona fide ace at the top of its rotation for about a decade. He sits fourth in team history in pitching WAR (43.1), but, overall, the support he received from his offense was historically uneven.

During his Phillies career, the team's bullpen blew 29 wins for him. Of his 90 losses with the team, 36 (40%) were in quality starts, sporting a 2.58 ERA in those losses. In fact, he went at least seven innings and allowed no more than two earned runs in 21 (23.3%) of the games *he* lost. In all, Hamels had 57 starts in which he went at least seven innings and allowed two or fewer runs, and did not *earn* a win; in 12 of these he did not allow a single earned run. He was 0–21 with a 1.63 ERA in those starts.

Hamels was 9–9 with a 2.46 ERA in 2014. This was the best season in terms of ERA by a pitcher with at least 30 starts and fewer than 10 wins since Tricky Nichols went 4–29 with a 2.38 ERA in 1875. Tricky had a 7.66 RA (ERA, but including unearned runs) that season. Hamels was 0–9, with a 3.04 ERA in the games he didn't win that season.

Final 70 starts with Phillies – 2.95 ERA & 21–21

Final 81 starts with Phillies – 3.04 ERA & 23–28

Final 100 starts with Phillies – 3.14 ERA & 30–33

Five Aces

The Phillies won a franchise-record 102 games in 2011, before exiting in the opening-round NLDS. Early playoff exits tend to mute regular season accomplishments, so it might be difficult to remember, or consider, that the Phillies may have fielded the greatest starting rotation of all time. Well, at least among five-man rotations. Maybe.

The five-man has roots that date back to the early part of last century, but it didn't become a staple of the game until the 1970s. In terms of ERA, the best rotation during the Live Ball Era (post-1919) was the 1981 Houston Astros' unit (2.43 ERA), but they're penalized by playing just 110 games during a strike-shortened season. The Phillies' 2011 quintet, featuring, predominantly, Roy Halladay (19–6, 2.35 ERA), Cliff Lee (17–8, 2.40 ERA), Cole

Hamels (14–9, 2.79 ERA), Vance Worley (11–3, 3.01 ERA), and Roy Oswalt (9–10, 3.69 ERA), ranks third during the five-man era (40th during Live Ball), and is the best in baseball since 1985.

That year, the Mets qualified as having the best five-man ERA (2.84), but they were top heavy, with Doc Gooden at his peak of complete domination (24–4, 1.53 ERA). The Phillies rank a tad behind at 2.86, but were deep and dangerous, top to bottom.

During the Live Ball Era, regardless of rotation size, the Phillies' Five ranks eighth in WHIP (1.110), and fifth in K/9 (7.9; NL record until 2014), with the very best strikeout-to-walk ratio (4.22). Of course, it's hard to quantify "best" and no one ever seems to agree on a team, or even method.

[What's In a Win? The 1971 Baltimore Orioles have often gotten the "best rotation" moniker, because they were just the second team since 1920 with four 20-game winners, but the 1972 O's actually had a better ERA (2.58 to 2.91), with the fourth-best WHIP of the Live Ball Era (1.094).]

For simplicity's sake, let's assume the Phillies fielded the best five-man rotation. And five is better than four. So . . . the 2011 Phillies had the greatest rotation of all time. Maybe.

STATS INCREDIBLE!

20: Consecutive games in which Pete Rose reached base safely multiple times, from September 3 to September 22, 1979. He batted .500/.589/.603 during that span.

19: Consecutive games in which Rose recorded a hit and did not strike out, from June 9 to June 27, 1982. No player has had a longer streak since.

70: In 1984, Juan Samuel had 70 extra-base hits and 72 stolen bases. He and Ty Cobb (1911) are the only players in baseball history to have 70+ extra-base hits and 70+ stolen bases in a season.

2: Home runs hit by starting pitcher Rick Wise during a June 23, 1971 blanking of the Reds, 4-0. Amazingly, Wise no-hit the Big Red Machine, turning in, arguably, the single most dominant performance by a player in baseball history.

7: Number of players in MLB history with 900+ extra-base hits and 400+ stolen bases. Among them are five Hall of Famers, Barry Bonds, and Phillies great Bobby Abreu.

5: Number of players with at least 2,400 hits, 1,400 walks, and 400 stolen bases—Bonds, Rickey Henderson, Joe Morgan, Eddie Collins, and Abreu.

9: Number of seasons in which Abreu had 60+ extra base hits and 20+ stolen bases—the most in baseball history.

4: Record number of players on one team with 60+ extra-base hits and 20+ stolen bases (Rollins, Utley, Shane Victorino, and Jayson Werth; 2009).

16: Home runs hit by Pat Burrell on three-ball counts in 2002, most in recorded history. His 12 full-count home runs that season are also a record.

238: Number of strikeouts by Cliff Lee in 2011, and he did not throw a single wild pitch that year. Lee collected the most strikeouts in a season in baseball history without a wild pitch. The following season he became the first pitcher with 200+ strikeouts and fewer than 30 walks since Cy Young in 1904. The season after that, he faced 876 batters—walking just one on four pitches.

147: On October 21, 1993, with the Phillies facing elimination, Curt Schilling shut out the Blue Jays on 147 pitches in Game 5 of the World Series. Schilling would go on to be one of the most clutch pitchers in postseason history, winning five of five starts with his teams facing elimination.

2,234: Career hits for Michael Jack Schmidt, of which 548 were home runs. His final hit, though, was a bunt single.

.400: Outfielders Ed Delahanty, Billy Hamilton, and Sam Thompson batted .401 from 1894 to 1895. They combined to go 1,218-for-3,039 over the two-season span. In 1894, the Phillies had four outfielders bat above .400—the aforementioned trio, in addition to the team's leading hitter that season, Tuck Turner.

66: Number of wins Robin Roberts fell shy of 300 career victories. Also the number of complete game losses he had in his career. Roberts also had 37 career starts in which he went at least eight innings, allowed no more than two runs (earned or unearned), and *lost*. This is the most during the Live Ball Era.

WASHINGTON NATIONALS

Est. 1969

EXPOS – *Vlad Guerrero and Tim Raines both averaged 4.474 WAR per 162 games played during their careers. Reggie Jackson averaged 4.240 WAR per 162 games played, and Derek Jeter 4.234.*

NATIONALS – *In 2015, Bryce Harper became the youngest player in baseball history with at least 40 homers and 120 walks in a season. The previous youngest was one George Herman "Babe" Ruth in 1920, the year that birthed the Live Ball Era.*

The Nationals have only been around for 11 years, so they still have that new-franchise smell. But baseball in the nation's capital is not a novel concept.

Professional baseball in D.C. dates back as far as 1872, with several short-lived iterations, such as the Olympics, Blue Legs, and even a few unaffiliated Nationals squads taking the field. Of course, the one with the most staying power was the Washington Senators, a charter American League franchise that played in D.C. for 60 years before shipping off and becoming the Twins of Minnesota in 1961. In its place, the franchise now known as the Texas Rangers tried its hand for a decade in D.C. (1961–71), also as the Washington Senators. It didn't work out.

The first Senators team slogan:

"First in war, first in peace, and last in the American League."

The second Senators team slogan:

"First in war, first in peace, and STILL last in the American League."

There's your reason why "Senators" maybe wasn't given much serious consideration when it came time to name the new one. If luck plays any role at all, it is probably a good omen that, instead of moving *out*, this was the first existing MLB franchise moving *in* to Washington.

The franchise began as the expansion Montreal Expos in 1969, the first MLB team located outside of the United States. From the onset, they were dreadful.

The Expos failed to reach .500 in any of their first ten seasons. In the 35 years they played in Montreal, their only successful campaigns of note came during the strike-shortened seasons of 1981 and 1994.

Nineteen eighty-one is the only year the Expos made the playoffs*—with an asterisk, however, because of a bizarre one-time rule that allowed them to advance with a second-place record.

In 1994, they finally had their first (and only) first-place finish—but, this time the strike lasted and there would be no playoffs to make.

Tragic.

The 1994 strike, famously, struck a damaging shot to the popularity of baseball everywhere. To the Montreal Expos specifically, it was a death blow.

By 2001, stadium attendance dropped to just 7,935 per game. The Seattle Mariners' attendance the same season was over five times higher (43,302 per game). The Florida Marlins, the next-to-worst draw in baseball, doubled Montreal's average (15,765). *Heck, even the Milwaukee Brewers' Triple-A affiliate Indianapolis Indians drew 578 more fans per game in 2001.* Yikes.

Major League Baseball took control of the club and eventually moved it to Washington in 2005. And after an Expos-esque rocky start, the Nationals have actually found a way to win with regularity—a novel concept for both the franchise and city.

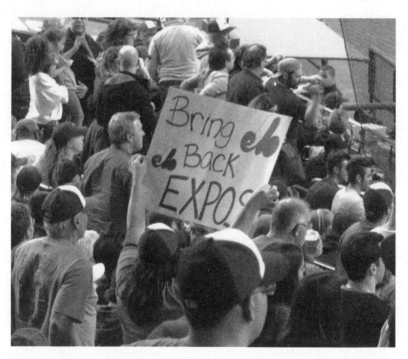

One fan's plea for the Expos' return, at an exhibition game between the Cincinnati Reds and Toronto Blue Jays, at Montreal's Olympic Stadium on April 3, 2015. (Resolute)

'Spos with the Most

Not coincidentally, three of the Expos' best players—Gary Carter, Andre Dawson, and Tim Raines—all played together during one of the franchise's best five-year stretches, from 1979–83.

Gary Carter *(C, 1974–84)*: Carter was the Expos' first Hall of Fame representative, and one of the best catchers of his generation. During the 11 years he was an Expo (1974–84), no catcher in the National League had more hits (1,365), doubles (256), triples (23), home runs (215), RBIs (794), runs scored (683), walks (549), or high-fives (many) than Carter. He was also a tremendous defensive player, leading the league in defensive WAR over the same span (20.9) while collecting three straight Gold Gloves, from 1980–82. In overall WAR per 162 games, Carter is tops among Expos with a 5.99 average.

Andre Dawson *(OF, 1976–86)*: Seven years after Gary Carter's induction, Dawson became the franchise's second, and last, Hall of Famer. He was a true double threat, averaging 20 home runs and 23 stolen bases during his 11 seasons in Montreal. During that stretch, from 1976–86, Dawson led the National League with five 20/20 seasons. No one else even had four. Dawson was the only player during the 1980s to collect 250+ homers and 150+ steals (250 HRs, 199 SBs).

Forget double threat, Dawson was a triple threat, winning six straight Gold Gloves with Montreal (1980–85) and eight overall. Among National League outfielders in the 1980s, Dawson was second to only Barry Bonds in total defensive WAR (4.9 to 6.9).

Tim Raines *(OF, 1979–90)*: "Rock" Raines, the franchise offensive WAR leader (47.5), isn't in the Hall of Fame *yet*. And it doesn't make any sense.

The speedster's calling card was the stolen base, and no one—not even the Man of Steal Rickey Henderson—*did it more consistently or more efficiently.* He is the only player in baseball history to steal at least 70 bases in six consecutive seasons, doing so from 1981–86. And his 84.7% success rate on stolen base attempts for his career is the best in baseball history (minimum 400 attempts). Rickey, who of course topped Rock in sheer stolen base numbers, was not quite as selective as Raines—the "Greatest of All Time" would have to return to baseball and steal 448 consecutive bases without being caught to pass Raines in stolen bases efficiency.

[*Rickey, if you are reading this . . . Challenge accepted?*]

From 1982–86, Raines had at least 30 doubles and 70 stolen bases each season. Prior to 1982, the last *single* 30/70 season was Ty Cobb's way back in 1915. In 1987, Raines failed to replicate his past five 30/70 seasons. But no matter, as Raines batted a mighty .330/.429/.526 with 50 stolen bases, making him the first player to bat at least .325/.425/.525 with 50 stolen bases since 1922 MVP George Sisler accomplished the feat. The only player with such a season since? Nineteen ninety AL MVP Rickey Henderson.

The .294 career hitter was also a whiz from the batter's box, reaching base safely 3,977 times in his career—more than 3,000 hit club Hall of Famers Tony Gwynn, Nap Lajoie, Lou Brock, and Roberto Clemente. His career .385 on-base percentage bests 63.3% of all Hall of Fame position players, including Willie Mays at .384. His .425 slugging percentage bests Rickey Henderson at .419. His 123 OPS+ bests 500 Home Run Club member Ernie Banks. And his 69.1 WAR tops a man whom many call the "greatest hitter of a generation"—Tony Gwynn, at 68.8.

Not persuaded yet? Of the 18,663 players (through 2015) to ever play baseball, Tim Raines is the only one to amass at least 100 triples, 150 homers, and 600 stolen bases. He did so handily, with 113 three-baggers, 170 big flies, and 808 thieveries.

According to Baseball-Reference.com, Lou Brock is the most similar player to Raines. Here's how the two measure up against each other in a few key offensive categories:

Raines vs. Brock

BA: Rock
OBP: Rock
SLG: Rock
OPS: Rock
TOB: Rock
HR: Rock
SB%: Rock
OPS+: Rock
WAR: Rock
HOF: **Brock**

Additionally, Lou Brock had a career-high .385 on-base percentage in 1971. That was Rock's career on-base percentage. Brock had a career-best 83.8 stolen base percentage in 1968, which falls short of Rock's career stolen base percentage of 84.7. In fact, Brock would have to return to baseball and steal 762 consecutive bases without being caught to pass Tim Raines in career stolen base efficiency. Now, this is in no way a knock of the Hall of Fame career of Lou Brock; however, we just feel as though Rock's *Hall of Fame* career was just that much better.

Need we say more? *(We will, anyway)*. But for now . . . Rock the Hall, 2017!

The Impaler

Vladimir Guerrero *(OF, 1996–2003)* came a bit later with Montreal, but may have been the franchise's most talented player.

He batted .324/.391/.590, averaging 33 home runs and 100 RBIs during his seven full seasons in Montreal (1997–2003). Throughout his 16-year MLB career, Guerrero was famous for his ability to hit *any* pitch *very* hard. If he could reach the ball, he could hit it out of the park. Despite routinely lunging for pitches way out of the zone, he made great contact, finishing second to only Albert Pujols in 30+ homer/ sub-75 strikeout seasons over the past 20 years (Pujols, 10; Vlad, 6).

The 173 home runs and .927 OPS he had in six seasons with the Angels are impressive, and should propel him toward first-ballot enshrinement in the Hall in 2017, but his start in Montreal was better. His 144 OPS+ through his first six Expos seasons is better than the starts of Manny Ramirez (141), Mike Schmidt (141), Miguel Cabrera (140), and Barry Bonds (138).

In 2002, Guerrero batted .336/.417/.593 with 39 homers, 364 total bases, and 40 stolen bases—one of just nine 360+ TB/ 40+ SB seasons in history. Vlad, Willie Mays (1957), and Larry Walker (1997) are the only players ever with a .333+ BA/ 33 HR/ 33 SB season.

Overall, Guerrero had four seasons with at least 200 hits and 30 home runs. Only Lou Gehrig had more, with seven.

He was a special player, and if Raines is inducted in 2017, Vlad's may eventually be just the third Expos cap immortalized in Cooperstown.

Nats' Bats . . . and Arms

The Nationals are enjoying some sustained success in Washington these days, finishing over .500 the last four seasons, and reaching the postseason twice after their two best finishes in franchise history (98 wins, 2012; 96 wins, 2014).

Former no. 1 overall draft pick Stephen Strasburg (54–37, 3.09 ERA) has had difficulty staying on the field, but when healthy, he's been one of the most dynamic pitchers in baseball. Strasburg has reached double-digit strikeouts without allowing multiple walks in 14 of his first 132 career games. Only Roger Clemens (17) and Corey Kluber (16) have more such games through 132 played. Moreover, Strasburg already has as many career seasons (4) with at least 150 strikeouts and a strikeout percentage of 25.0% or better as Roger Clemens.

The rotation as a whole was the star in 2014, as Strasburg, Doug Fister, Jordan Zimmermann, Gio Gonzalez, and Tanner Roark combined for a 2.92 ERA. The Cubs, Tigers, Astros, Royals, Diamondbacks, Orioles, Blue Jays, Mets, and Brewers all didn't have a *single* pitcher with a qualified ERA as low as the Nats' rotation collective.

On the offensive side, super-young superstar Bryce Harper is the current face of the franchise, and, Nationals fans pray, will continue to be so for the next couple decades.

The twenty-two-year-old outfielder batted .330/.460/.649 in 2015—the youngest to slash at least that in a qualified season since Levi Meyerle in 1871. Harper is one of only three players in league history to lead the NL in home runs before turning twenty-three (Eddie Mathews, twenty-one; Johnny Bench, twenty-two). His 97 home runs to date are the fourth-most by a player through his age-twenty-two season, two more than Alex Rodriguez had at the same age.

In 2015, Bryce Harper (twenty-two; .330, 42 HRs) became the youngest player to bat at least .330 in a season with 40 homers since Joe DiMaggio in 1937 (twenty-two; .346, 46 HRs). DiMaggio was about five weeks younger than Harper. (Kevin Durso)

Harper already has a better WAR season (9.9, 2015) than the career highs of both Hank Aaron (9.4, 1961) and Ken Griffey Jr. (9.7, 1996), and, through his four seasons, he's got the *exact same* OPS and OPS+ as Aaron had through his first four (.902 OPS, 143 OPS+). Harper's historic 2015 makes him the youngest player to lead the majors in both on-base percentage and slugging percentage since Stan Musial in 1943. Stan repeated the feat in 1944, then enlisted in the US Navy in 1945. Tough act for the kid to follow.

Still think Mike Trout might be the best young player in the game today? Thus far, Harper has posted better career highs than Trout in batting average, on-base percentage, slugging percentage, OPS, OPS+, walks, and home runs.

A heck of a start. If things go according to plan, Harper just might finish by passing guys like Griffey, Rodriguez, Aaron, and maybe even Barry Bonds, in a slew of key offensive categories.

STATS INCREDIBLE!

158: The Montreal record for career wins, by Expos pitcher Steve Rogers. Ironically, also the civilian name of Captain *America*.

3: The number of players in baseball history with multiple seasons of at least 50 XBHs and 70 SBs. Ty Cobb had two, Rickey Henderson had two, and Tim Raines had four . . . consecutive.

7: The number of players in baseball history with at least 600 XBHs and 700 SBs. Among them, Tim Raines is the only player still awaiting his "Call to the Hall."

3: The number of seasons with at least 50 XBHs and 90 SBs in baseball history, two of which occurred during the 1800s: Pete Browning in 1887, Tom Brown in 1891, and Tim Raines in 1983.

91: Team-record total go-ahead home runs Vladimir Guerrero had with Montreal, 13 more than Andre Dawson and 23 more than Gary Carter.

0: The number of pitchers Bryce Harper faced that were younger than him, through four minor league levels and his first three MLB seasons.

1.109: Harper's OPS for the 2015 season. He is the youngest player with a season OPS of 1.100+ since Joe Kelley in 1894. He is the youngest player to lead the league in OBP (.460) and homers (42) since Ty Cobb in 1909 (.431 OBP, 9 HRs).

.649: Harper's slugging percentage in 2015. He's the youngest player with a SLG% that high since Joe DiMaggio in 1937.

506: The number of players selected before the Expos took Tom Brady in the 1995 MLB Draft. The New England Patriots selected him 199th overall in the 2000 NFL Draft.

8.2: In the 2014 18-inning NLDS Game 2 Giants win over the Nats (2–1), Jordan Zimmermann became the first pitcher ever to leave a postseason game with a shutout intact with two outs in the ninth inning.

86.6%: Career stolen base percentage of Nats outfielder Jayson Werth, second in baseball history to only Chase Utley's 88.8% (minimum 100 attempts).

NATIONAL LEAGUE CENTRAL

CHICAGO CUBS

Est. 1871

In 2015, Kris Bryant had 99 RBIs, the most by a Cubs rookie since Charles Irwin had a franchise rookie record 100 RBIs in 1894.

Today, the Cubbies are our lovable losers. At the start of it all, this could not have been foreseen.

Not to be confused with the crosstown White Sox, the Chicago White Stockings (they wouldn't be the "Cubs" until 1903) were there at the very beginning of organized baseball. They came together in 1871, and were charter members of the original National Association that eventually became the National League in 1876. The White Stockings, perhaps the most talented early franchise, added two very influential players in team, and baseball, history that first year—Al Spalding and Cap Anson.

Spalding was 252–65 over the course of his seven-year career (yep, that's 36 wins per year), but don't get too excited. He played in the age of underhand pitching, when called strikes were sometimes a mere suggestion, and the batters could announce where they wished the incoming pitch to be located. It's a natural evolutionary path for such a nuanced game, but it's important to remember, by modern standards, they were playing something like middle-school gym class softball. Still, Spalding was the best, and his .795 career winning percentage, in some circles, counts and is still a major-league record. But, his playing career doesn't even begin to explain his influence on the game.

He is still relevant today because of the sporting goods company he founded in Chicago that bears his name. He was one of the first players to use a glove in the field, and became one of the most influential visionaries in supplying what would quickly become a booming sporting goods market. To be fair, he's also the alleged architect of the unsubstantiated claim that Abner Doubleday invented the game, and that its birth was in Cooperstown, New York. Great stories sell product, and that was perhaps his motive. Great players, though, can also do the trick.

Cap Anson, Spalding's teammate and fellow Hall of Famer, was certainly one of the game's greatest, and most influential, players. His 27 seasons in Major League Baseball are still a record (tied with Nolan Ryan), and he was the very first member of the 3,000 hit club—even considering the fact that a variety of wild factors (in 1887, walks counted as hits) have Major League Baseball (3,081), MLB.com (3,011), and Baseball-Reference (3,435) all in disagreement over his actual hits total. His 20-year run as player/manager with Chicago saw the club win five pennants and reach two pre-modern era World Series. There was a tradition of success with Chicago baseball, and that continued into the 1900s.

No team was more successful during the first decade of the World Series era (1903) than the Cubs. From 1903–12, the team averaged 98 wins and 53 losses, for a .648 total winning percentage, which is higher than the Philadelphia Phillies have ever had for any one single season in their 133-year history. The Cubs appeared in half of the first eight World Series (1906–08, 1910), and were the first team with multiple wins (1907–08).

From here, things took a turn for the worse—for 107 years, and counting. The Cubs haven't won a World Series since 1908, and, somehow, a goat is to blame.

You can take your pick of goats—traditional (fan, Steve Bartman, *maybe* interfering on a play that would have helped get the Cubs to the World Series in 2003), or literal (the "Curse of the Billy Goat" story about a man damning the Cubs after being forced to leave the game . . . with his goat). Either way, it's hard to win a World Series, and some team has to have the longest professional championship drought—it might as well be the team with the best, most tolerant fans.

Over the years, iconic names have passed through Chicago's North Side, coming and going without a ring. From Grover Cleveland Alexander (named after President Cleveland, and later portrayed in a movie by Ronald Reagan) and Hack Wilson, to Ernie Banks, Ryne Sandberg, and Sammy Sosa. Fans still pack Wrigley Field regardless, as the Cubs have only once finished in the bottom half of NL attendance rankings since 1983, and haven't finished among the bottom two since 1966. The field probably has something to do with it.

Considered among baseball's few *cathedrals,* Wrigley is a spectacle, and a throwback to an age that represents not only baseball's infancy, but the dawn of American sports culture overall. It opened in 1914 (originally, Weeghman Park) and, with a few exceptions, has managed to keep its traditions intact, even if its most iconic feature—the outfield ivy—wasn't added until a renovation in 1937. Fans love it, within city limits and beyond, as Wrigley is one of the nation's must-sees for any eager baseball fan. In consideration of total entertainment value, perhaps the experience trumps the team's performance.

The ChiFeds of the Federal League, playing during the inaugural season of Weeghman Park, famously known later as Wrigley Field. (Author unknown. 1914 US postcard.)

2014 Wrigley Field, Cubs vs. Reds, 100 years later. (Daniel Betts)

Either way, it would be a mistake to downplay the Cubs' commitment to win again. The franchise returned to the playoffs for the first time in seven years last season, and looks eager to give its fans something else to love about their Cubbies—a new, winning tradition.

"Baseball's Sad Lexicon"

The famed "Tinker to Evers to Chance" double-play infield highlighted those successful Cubs squads of the early 1900s, made famous by the poem, "Baseball's Sad Lexicon," by Franklin Pierce Adams (when poetry was still a thing). (Joe) Tinker, (Johnny) Evers, and (Frank) Chance were all career sub-.790 OPS players, but Hall of Famers, still—the Cubbies were that infamous.

Shortstop Tinker still ranks tops in franchise history in defensive WAR (29.7), more than the second and third-ranked Cubs combined (Billy Jurges, 15.1; Ned Williamson, 13.1). He batted just .266/.307/.391 in 1908, but still registered a higher WAR that season (7.9) than Sammy Sosa did during his famous 66-homer MVP campaign in 1998 (6.4).

Evers is tied with fellow second baseman Ryne Sandberg for the fourth-highest career defensive WAR in team history (12.8), and was a decent, if unspectacular, .270/.356/.334 career hitter. Chance, however, picked up the offensive slack, batting .297/.394/.395, and, in franchise WAR, ranks as the Cubs' top first baseman of the modern era (45.5).

Mr. Cub

Ernie Banks was no borderline Hall of Famer. Arguably the franchise's greatest player, Banks redefined the shortstop position. With apologies to Joe Tinker, Banks was a beast.

The 19-year lifetime Cub (1953–71) ranks first in franchise history in extra-base hits (1,009) and second in home runs (512), and RBIs (1,636). Banks was the Cubs' first black player to appear in a game, and was one of baseball's first shortstops to break the mold at his position (even though he played more career games at first base . . . never matter).

Banks was the first member of the 500 home run club to spend significant time at shortstop, and was actually the very first shortstop to hit even 250. He had four straight 40+ home run seasons from 1957–60, while former National League home run champs Hank Aaron and Willie Mays never had more than two straight. Four times he led the league in extra-base hits, again besting Mays (2) and current home run king, Barry Bonds (3).

At the time of his retirement in 1971, Banks ranked tops all-time in home runs as a shortstop (277), which was just 54.1% of his career 512 homers.

Slammin' Sammy

Sammy Sosa's nickname is a fun homonym that works both as an ode to his tremendous home run production, and as a bashing, or slam, of his character.

Alleged steroid use aside, the controversial Cubs outfielder had one of the greatest offensive runs in baseball history. Through

Major League Baseball's first 122 years (1876–1997), only one player hit as many as 61 home runs in a single season (Roger Maris; 61, 1961). Then, over a four-year stretch, from 1998–2001, Sosa *averaged* 61 homers. His 1.058 OPS during that period is higher than any one single-season OPS from Hall of Fame outfielders Willie Stargell, Rickey Henderson, or Reggie Jackson.

He's the top home run hitter in franchise history (545), and is third in RBIs (1,414). His 609 bombs overall are good for eighth in MLB history. And he owes it all to a sudden, tremendous uptick in production during the second half of his career.

Through his first nine seasons, Sosa averaged a per-162 game average of 31 home runs and 96 RBIs. His final nine seasons, the slugger bumped those per-162 averages to 52 home runs and 132 RBIs.

He owns 37.5% of all 60-home run seasons in baseball history (3 of 8), and that figure is unlikely to change anytime soon, as the game has since shifted into a decidedly pitching-friendly age.

Jake Arrieta

Speaking of sudden dominance, Jake Arrieta's mastery on the mound for Chicago in 2015 was almost supernatural.

Arrieta had never qualified for an ERA title in any of his five previous seasons before blowing up last year, going 22–6 with a 1.77 ERA. The last Cubs pitcher with at least a 1.77 ERA and 4.92 strikeout-to-walk ratio was Fred Goldsmith in 1880. Arrieta's was just the 10th qualified ERA season that low since 1998, but it's what the twenty-nine-year-old right-hander did down the stretch that sets him apart from all the rest.

The 2015 Cy Young winner's 0.75 ERA in the second half was the lowest ERA for any half in baseball history. He went 12–1 during that stretch, surrendering just nine earned runs in 107.1

innings. Former Cubs teammate Jeff Samardzija had *three starts* with at least nine earned runs surrendered last season.

Jake does it at the plate, too. From 2014 to 2015, he has hit for extra-bases at a greater rate (5.51%) than he has allowed them to opponents (5.13%).

STATS INCREDIBLE!

1943: Third baseman Kris Byant was the first Cubs rookie to start and bat cleanup in his major-league debut since Heinz Becker on April 21, 1943.

2: In 2015, Kris Bryant became the first Cubs rookie with multiple walk-off home runs in a season since Gabby Hartnett in 1923 (2, each).

15: Last season, Bryant and outfielder Kyle Schwarber, clubbing 26 and 16 home runs, respectively, became the first two players in club history with 15+ home runs in their first MLB season.

2.26: Jake Arrieta's FIP (fielding independent pitching) in 2014—the best by a Cubs pitcher with at least 150 innings since Grover Cleveland Alexander in 1919.

1876: The National League's founding year. In 2015, Kris Bryant and Kyle Schwarber became the first NL rookie teammates to each have an OBP of at least .355 with 15+ home runs.

151: Sammy Sosa's OPS+ in 1999, and Wade Boggs's OPS+ with Boston in 1985. Sosa hit 63 home runs, while Boggs hit just 8.

163: Average games played per season by Cubs Hall of Famer Billy Williams, over a five-year stretch, from 1965–69. In fact, he averaged 162.25 games played from 1963–70.

4: The amount of seasons Ernie Banks had a 7.5+ WAR—more than Sosa (1) and Derek Jeter (2), combined.

120: Cap Anson's RBI total as a member of the Colts/Cubs in 1891. At thirty-nine years old, he's the oldest player in baseball history to lead the league.

.339: Hall of Fame catcher Gabby Hartnett batted at least this high for three separate seasons during his 19-year Cubs career (1922–40). No other catcher during the modern era had more than two such seasons.

1896: On July 29, 2014, backup catcher John Baker took the mound for the Cubs in the 16th inning, making him the first Cub to pitch and catch in the same season since Malachi Kittridge in 1896.

The 1906 Cubs, featuring the famed double-play unit, Tinker, Evers, and Chance. (George Lawrence Company)

CINCINNATI REDS

Est. 1881

The 1975 World Champion Reds are the only Live Ball Era (post-1919) team on which every pitcher had a winning record.

Funny story: The franchise, known early on as the Red Stockings, got its start because of a weird exile of the former National League Cincinnati Reds—a totally unaffiliated franchise. Why did the NL Reds get booted? They were selling beer during games, and playing on Sundays. *SACRILEGE!*

Crazy, but rules are rules, right?

Well . . .

The Reds hadn't actually broken any at the time of their ousting. While the drinking and sabbath rules would eventually go into effect soon after, the Reds, at the time, had merely broken a gentlemen's agreement. Either way, it was enough to get the franchise voted out prior to the 1881 season.

By 1882, the Red Stockings of Cincinnati surfaced in the new American Association, eventually joining the National League in 1890, as the Reds—shiny and new. They are the oldest one-city, continuously-operating franchise in Major League Baseball.

The Reds had a rough go of it early on, never finishing higher than third place in any of the club's first 29 years in the NL

(1890–1918)—and they only finished that high on four separate occasions.

Hall of Famer Edd Roush led the Reds in 1919 to their first championship—but even that was dubious. The Reds were good, but their opponent, the Chicago White Sox, were a *great* club, which just amplified the evidence that certain Chicago players conspired to throw the Series (see *Black Sox Scandal*; Chicago White Sox). It's one of those rare World Series championships in that it just *kinda-sorta* counts—which made 1940 so important.

That season, Cincinnati won its first controversy-free championship, with a solid, if unspectacular, squad led by the league's best player, Bucky Walters.

Walters isn't exactly a household name, but he's in good company with all-time greats like Cy Young, Walter Johnson, and Sandy Koufax, as Walters won pitching's Triple Crown in 1939, with an NL-best 27 wins, 2.29 ERA, and 137 strikeouts. In 1940 (22 Ws, 2.48 ERA, 115 Ks), Walters finished just 12 strikeouts short of a second straight Crown, but the World Series ring was probably a suitable substitute.

The Reds fell back to mediocrity soon after, winning just one pennant, with a fifth-place average finish, over the following 29 years. They weren't bad—Hall of Famer Frank Robinson had some of his best years during his decade with the team (1956–65), but the Reds struggled to build around him. As it turned out, they ended up building a juggernaut *without* him.

Cincinnati's farm system produced All-Stars Pete Rose (1963), Tony Perez (1964), and Johnny Bench (1967) in the 1960s, bolstering the Reds' offense, even with the departure of Robinson in 1966. By 1970, with new skipper Sparky Anderson at the helm, the new-look Reds generation was starting to take shape. Cincinnati was suddenly bigger, redder, and . . . *machinier*.

The Big Red Machine

The Reds made it back to the World Series in 1970, a losing effort to the Baltimore Orioles (4-1). Over the next six years, however, the Reds would play in three more, winning two, while cementing a legacy as one of the greatest collections of talent in baseball history: *The Big Red Machine.*

Sure, **Frank Robinson** was a huge loss in 1966. To date, only four Reds (just once apiece) have had a .300+ batting average, 30+ homer, 100+ RBI season since Robinson *averaged* .303/32 HRs/101 RBIs for his entire 10-year Reds career. The team maybe never replaced him, man-for-man, but they certainly overcompensated, peppering nearly every position with Hall of Fame-caliber talent.

Pete Rose, a.k.a. "Charlie Hustle," a.k.a. "Hit King," a.k.a. "That Guy Banned from Baseball" (never mind that), was the centerpiece of the Machine. He was already well-established by 1970, coming off two straight batting titles, and averaging 204 hits the previous five years. Barry Bonds never had more than 181 hits in any single season.

There were times during his 24-year career when he was the best—three-time batting champion, seven-time league leader in hits, 17-time All-Star, and 1973 NL MVP—but Rose's legacy was in his ability to outplay, outlast, and out-hustle pretty much every other player to ever step onto the field. He never batted .400 (or even .350), or swatted 50 homers (or even 20), but he was consistent. *Every. Single. Day.*

He reached base safely in 2,993 games in his career, and only seven other players in history have even played that many—Willie Mays, with 2,992, is not one of them.

The all-time hit king finished with 4,256 for his career—more than the top 17 hits totals in MLB history combined.

Rose was the kind of player every team likes to build around—a "Moneyball" guy that, even when sporting a poor batting average, could still produce. He batted just .272 in his forties, but with it, a better on-base percentage (.354) than Dave Winfield had during his entire career (.353).

Rose had three seasons with at least 150 singles, 50 extra-base hits, and 75 walks. Wade Boggs (4) is the only player ever with more. No other player had even two. Rose's six seasons with at least 150 singles and 50 extra-base hits are the most all-time.

Tony Perez and **Johnny Bench** were the other holdovers from the '60s to make up the offensive machine. Perez's career numbers aren't astounding for his position (.279 BA, 379 HRs in 23 years), but he led all National League first basemen in homers in the 1970s (226) with almost 200 more RBIs (954) than any other first bagger. He wasn't an all-timer, but he was best for his time. Bench, on the other hand, was just a flat-out rock star.

While Mike Piazza has the most home runs by primary catchers (427), Bench (389), with a 75.0 career WAR, blows away Piazza (59.4) and every other catcher in history, in the WAR category. He's one of only five catchers ever with a 40-homer season, and he did it twice, setting the all-time single-season record for his position in the process (45; 1970).

Across all positions, Bench was second to only Willie Stargell in NL home runs during the 1970s, and was the only player in the game to accumulate 1,000+ RBIs during the decade (1,013).

Second baseman **Joe Morgan** was the final major cog in the Big Red Machine—with due respect to nine-time All-Star, and five-time Gold Glove shortstop Dave Concepción; 1977 NL MVP George Foster, whose 52 home runs and 149 RBIs that season were both MLB highs for the decade; or Ken Griffey Sr. who, in 1976, became just the second player in Reds history to bat .330+ with 30+ stolen bases (.336 BA, 34 SBs) . . . Too much talent, not enough pages.

Morgan turned out to be the difference maker, landing in Cincinnati via trade in 1972, taking the Reds' production, and his own career, to new levels.

Until that point, Morgan was just a .263/.375/.396 hitter in nine years with Houston. The next eight years with Cincy, Morgan won five Gold Gloves, and MVPs in back-to-back seasons (1975–76), doing things that 5-7, 160-lb middle infielders aren't supposed to do.

Literally, Morgan (1976) and Hack Wilson (1929–30) are the only two players under 68-inches tall to record a 1.000 OPS season. And Morgan is the lightest player to ever do it. Since 1903, only two players under five-foot-eight—Morgan and Paul Waner— have had a .435+ on-base percentage season. *And Morgan averaged .438 over a four-year span, from 1974–77.*

Taking size out of it, Morgan was still a very unique player. In his career, he had four seasons with 50+ extra-base hits, 50+ stolen bases, and 100+ walks. Every other player in baseball history combined have . . . ZERO. Over four seasons, from 1972-76, Little Joe averaged a mammoth 10.41 WAR per 162 games played. Hammerin' Hank Aaron had a heck of a career, but he never had a WAR that high in any single one of his 23 seasons.

The Big Red Machine averaged 98 wins per season from 1970– 76, winning titles in back-to-back seasons—the last NL squad to do so—in 1975 and 1976, Morgan's MVP seasons.

By 1980, the Machine was effectively dismantled. Only Bench, Concepción, Foster, and Griffey remained of the "Great Eight," and the franchise wouldn't win another title until a a ragtag group of new kids took home the hardware in 1990.

The Nasty Boys

It's both correct and incorrect to call the 1990 squad the first Reds team since 1979 to finish in first place. In 1981, Cincy finished with the best record in baseball, but a mid-season strike shortened play, and split the season into two independent halves. The leaders of each half moved on to the playoffs. Even though the Reds had the best record in baseball, they didn't lead after either half, and thus didn't participate in the playoffs. Dumb? Yep. Moving on . . .

The 1990 Reds were a club that was probably greater than the sum of its parts. Aside from Silver Slugger-winning shortstop Barry Larkin, the team was rather benign on offense. Jose Rijo (14–8, 2.70 ERA) and Jack Armstrong (12–9, 3.42 ERA) led a decent rotation, but the real difference maker was the bullpen—heck, even the NLCS MVPs were Reds pen mates, Rob Dibble and Randy Myers, who surrendered zero runs and just two hits to the Pirates in 10.2 innings.

The bullpen, more specifically Dibble (1.74 ERA), Myers (2.08), and Norm Charlton (3.02 in relief), referred to themselves as the *Nasty Boys*, and their offerings certainly reflected the moniker.

Dibble (136 Ks) and Myers (98 Ks) finished 1–2 in baseball in relief strikeouts. In the National League, no bullpen duo had a better combined ERA (1.90). Unfortunately, it proved unsustainable.

Dibble had more 100+ strikeout, sub-100 inning seasons (4) than anyone in baseball history, and had a phenomenal 1.82 ERA and .185 batting average against over his first 200 games. But, injuries would limit his MLB career to just seven seasons. While Myers pitched a full career, his ERA was a pedestrian 3.56 in eight seasons after 1990.

The '90 squad may have been a flash in the pan, but Larkin sure wasn't.

Larkin to Votto

Barry Larkin (1986–2004), a lifetime Red, played during the heart of the steroid era. While he won nine Silver Sluggers and an MVP, while making 12 All-Star teams, the last quarter of his career seemed to be a showcase of shortstops flexing their muscles.

Whether inflated by steroid use or not, Larkin's career numbers were getting dwarfed by power-hitting shortstops like Alex Rodriguez and Miguel Tejada early in the 2000s. Larkin, a seemingly clean player, maybe because of this, was not a first-ballot Hall of Famer. But he could have been.

Barry Larkin's display at the National Baseball Hall of Fame. At the center, his 1995 NL MVP Award. (Kevin Durso)

Among players that just played shortstop, Larkin has the third-highest career WAR in baseball history (70.2). During a four-year stretch, from 1995–98, Larkin maintained a .921 OPS. Up to that point in the National League, Woody English, Arky Vaughn, Ernie Banks, and Honus Wagner were the only shortstops to put up an OPS that high in a single season. That's good company.

In Larkin's 19-year career, he only twice played in the postseason. First baseman Joey Votto, a current nine-year Red, has three trips so far, but no rings. It hasn't been his fault.

Votto is one of the best hitters in the game today, but it's what he does keeping the bat on his shoulder that puts him in the all-time categories.

Much to the chagrin of *some* Reds fans, Votto has averaged just 24 home runs and 77 RBIs through his first eight full seasons, but he's proven to have one of the best eyes in the game. Four of the past five years, Votto has led the league in walks. In 2011, he did it while only playing in 111 games (94 BBs). It's the highest walk total in league history among players who appeared in 111 or fewer games.

Votto had one of his best seasons in 2015 (.314/.459/.541; 143 BBs), becoming the only player this millennium not named Barry Bonds to have a 140-walk season. Still, the Reds sputtered to just 64 wins. He's signed with the club for nine more years, so it will be interesting to see if they make Votto the centerpiece of a new offensive steamroller, or just continue to surround him with spare parts.

STATS INCREDIBLE!

1939: The year Frank McCormick (18 HRs, 16 Ks) and Ernie Lombardi (20 HRs, 19 Ks) became the first and only pair of teammates in NL history to each have more home runs than strikeouts.

189: The career strikeout total of former NL MVP and eight-time All-Star, McCormick. Cubs rookie Kris Bryant had 199 during last season alone.

.154: Opponents' batting average against Reds closer Aroldis Chapman. It's the lowest career batting average against in baseball history.

100.3: Average speed (MPH) of a Chapman fastball in 2014.

105.1: MPH of a Chapman fastball on September 24, 2010, against the San Diego Padres. It's the fastest verified pitch in history.

[Also, Cincinnati's Country Music Station, B-105.1]

106: Batters struck out by Chapman over 54 innings in 2014. It's the best season K% (52.5%) and K/9 (17.67) in history among pitchers with at least 50 innings.

100/100: The Pete Rose–managed 1987 Reds are the only team in history with 100 home runs and 100 stolen bases from outfielders (102 HRs, 120 SBs).

115: Runs scored by Rose in 1973. He was not thrown out at home once.

490: Career hits by Rose off of would-be Hall of Fame pitchers. He batted .303 against them.

224: Rose had 224 more multi-hit games (1,225) than no-hit games (1,001) in his career. Among those 1,001 games in which he failed to hit safely, he reached base safely in 432 of them.

2: Number of seasons Joey Votto has accumulated 20+ home runs with 135+ walks. Only Barry Bonds, Ted Williams, and Babe Ruth have done it more.

2-2-1: On June 23, 2014, Devin Mesoraco became the first player during the Live Ball Era with two walks, two hit-by-pitch, and a home run, all in the same game.

16: Sam Crawford's MLB-leading home run total in 1901. A dozen of them were inside-the-park.

50/100: In 697 plate appearances, from May 27, 1986 to July 10, 1987, Eric Davis had 50 home runs and 100 stolen bases. Perspective: Derek Jeter averaged 697 plate appearances from 1996–2012.

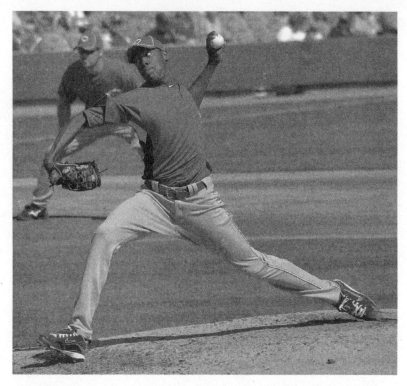

Aroldis Chapman, unfurling one of the most powerful deliveries in the game's history. (Flickr SD Dirk, CC BY 2.0)

MILWAUKEE BREWERS

Est. 1969

In 2013, Carlos Gomez and Jean Segura became the first teammates with at least 20 doubles, 10 triples, 10 home runs, and 40 stolen bases each since Jimmy Bannon and Hugh Duffy in 1894.

Milwaukee lost the Braves in 1966, and seemed like a good candidate for an expansion team in 1969. Instead, Seattle was awarded the designation, where the Pilots spent just one single season. But, Milwaukee and an ownership group headed by Bud Selig were persistent.

Financial woes killed the Pilots after just one season, and Milwaukee pounced in the eleventh hour, officially obtaining the franchise with just six days to go until Opening Day. To their credit, the Brewers group was prepared, but it's hard to imagine a team could pull this off today. Imagine selling the public on a new baseball team, a week before the start of the season, that doesn't yet exist. Uniforms were the only real concession, as the Brewers basically had to go with a simple variant of the Pilots jersey, with a color scheme that remained essentially unchanged for years.

The Brewers have been a success in Milwaukee, in the sense that the team is still there. From a competitiveness standpoint, it has been a struggle.

Aside from several respectable spurts of competitiveness, the Brewers have only made the postseason four times, with just one league championship in their history. On the bright side, Miller Park looks to be one of the true success stories in new stadium construction, and a real asset for Milwaukee.

In Milwaukee's 15 seasons at Miller Park, it has finished at least in the top half, or better, in league attendance when finishing over .500. That wasn't always the case at County Stadium. In the ten seasons in which the Brewers finished over .500 in their old digs, they only finished in the top half in league attendance rankings five times. Surely, when the Brewers have been able to put talent on the field, the public has responded favorably.

The Brewers' best run came during a six-year stretch, from 1978–83, as they made two postseason appearances, including one trip to the World Series (1982; L – St. Louis Cardinals), while compiling a .564 win percentage (91–71 per 162 games). Hall of Famers and 3,000 hit club members **Robin Yount** *(SS, OF, 1974–93)* and **Paul Molitor** *(3B, 1978–92)*, highlighted those Brewers squads, but they never sealed the deal.

Currently, the Brewers have much different uniforms, a new venue, and even a new league (NL, since 1998), but they've enjoyed recent runs that hearken back to the "glory" days. In 2011, they won a franchise-best 96 games, and, despite a very disappointing finish last season, they have one of the best centerpieces in baseball in six-time All-Star Ryan Braun.

AL Brew Crew

Robin Yount (shortstop/centerfield) and Paul Molitor (third base) are the only two Brewers representatives in the Hall of Fame, and spent a combined 35 years with the organization, 15 of which they shared, playing together from 1978–92.

Yount finished his 20-year career, start-to-finish in Milwaukee, in rare company. He is one of just five players in history with 3,000+ hits, 250+ home runs, and 250+ stolen bases, along with just Craig Biggio, Derek Jeter, Rickey Henderson, and Willie Mays.

The two-time MVP is one of just four players (Hank Greenberg, Stan Musial, Alex Rodriguez) to win the award at multiple positions (shortstop, outfield). Yount (583) and Baltimore's Cal Ripken Jr. (603) are the only primary shortstops in baseball history with over 550 career doubles.

Where Yount stands very much alone is in franchise history, as he ranks first in games played (2,856), runs scored (1,632), hits (3,142), total bases (4,730), doubles (583), and triples (126)—all categories in which Molitor ranks second.

It wasn't that Molitor was necessarily a lesser player than Yount—certainly, the case could be made both ways—but he simply didn't play as long in Milwaukee. Molitor's career overall was pretty special.

Only Barry Bonds, Ty Cobb, and Honus Wagner (heard of 'em?) join Molitor in the 900+ extra-base hit/ 500+ stolen base club. He was not much of a power guy, slugging just 160 home runs during his 15-year Milwaukee career, but he didn't need to be. Instead, Molitor built a Hall of Fame career as a doubles hitter.

No one hit more doubles than Molitor over a 10-year stretch, from 1987–96 (344), and, in 1987 particularly, Molitor led the league with 41 doubles, despite playing just 118 games due to injury.

The versatile infielder/DH hit 114 triples and 234 home runs, while stealing 504 bases in his career. No other player in history has more of each.

NL Brew Crew

Milwaukee, which was home to the NL Braves for 13 seasons (1953–65), opted to switch its Brewers to the National League in 1998, after the expansion Tampa Bay Devil Rays and Arizona Diamondbacks created an odd number of teams in each league. While this is not a problem today, Major League Baseball, at the time, was still protecting intraleague play.

The NL version of the Brewers didn't finish over .500 until 2008, but, once over the hump, they had a decent run, with some of the game's best players.

First baseman Prince Fielder, the heaviest position player in team history (275 lbs), played for seven years in Milwaukee (2005–11). He started with a splash, averaging 40 home runs his first four full seasons. His 50 home runs in 2007 is a Brewers franchise record. And combined with his father's 51-homer campaign in 1990, make the Fielder family the only father-son duo to each hit for 50 home runs in a season. *[Made you think . . . Bobby Bonds topped out at 39 homers in 1973 and Ken Griffey Sr. hit his career-high of 21 in 1986.]*

Perhaps Milwaukee was fearful of his bulky free agent price tag, and/or frame, but Fielder was not re-signed following the 2011 season, leaving just one superstar remaining in the Milwaukee batter's box.

Ryan Braun, the lifetime Brewer, signed through 2021, won the Rookie of the Year in 2007 and the league MVP in 2011. The slugger's had bumps in the road with performance-enhancing drug (PED) usage, but on or off the juice, he is still one of the game's elite.

He batted .324/.370/.634 with 34 home runs his first season, setting the all-time rookie mark for slugging percentage and becoming just the fourth player ever with a 1.000+ OPS in his very

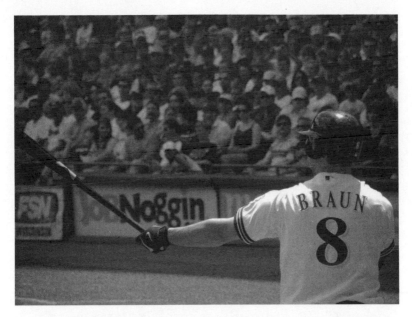

Ryan Braun was the 2007 Rookie of the Year. (Steve Paluch, CC BY 2.0)

first year (minimum 100 games). He was the fifth-fastest player in history to hit his 25th homer (82 games).

Braun has yet to eclipse *all* those rookie highs, but following up his 2007 with five straight Silver Sluggers is quite an encore. He and Darryl Strawberry are the only players in baseball history to begin their career with six straight seasons with 25+ home runs and 10+ stolen bases.

Most importantly, the Brewers have finished over .500 in five of Braun's eight full seasons. The NL squad never finished over the hump until Braun's rookie season. The first Jewish MVP since 1963 hasn't always been a mensch, but his production has certainly been a mitzvah for Milwaukee baseball fans.

STATS INCREDIBLE!

11: Total Milwaukee Brewers to reach double-digit steal totals in 1992, a single-season modern era record.

8: Consecutive games, from August 20, 2012 to August 28, 2012, in which the Brewers struck out double-digit batters, the longest streak in MLB history.

565: The combined weight, in pounds, of teammates Prince Fielder and C. C. Sabathia (2008). Per official weight records, the two are the heaviest hitter-pitcher combo in major-league history.

2: The amount of four-hit games by Robin Yount during the 1982 World Series. He's the only player with multiple four-hit World Series games for a *career*.

.095: Jim Abbott, in his offensive career (24 PAs in 1999), had three sac bunts, two hits, and three RBIs, batting .095/.095/.095. All of his hits and RBIs came off of Jon Lieber. He also pitched a no-hitter for the Yankees in 1993, despite the challenge of having been born with no right hand.

2: Number of career inside-the-park home runs for Prince Fielder (275+ lbs), exactly twice as many as the stolen base king, Rickey Henderson, had.

430: Batters faced by Ben Sheets in 2006. He fell behind just nine of them, 3–0. He came back to strike out four while walking just one.

PITTSBURGH PIRATES

Est. 1882

Roberto Clemente batted .328/.369/.488 with 104 runs, 201 hits, 35 doubles, nine triples, 15 home runs, 102 runs batted in, one stolen base, 11 outfield assists, and just one error during the final 162 games of his career.

Baseball's modern era (beginning 1900) is such an important distinction in baseball history. Before this time, the critical rules of the game were still being defined.

For much of Pittsburgh's early years, it mired in mediocrity, never finishing in first place in any pre-modern era season. History gives the team a pass, however, as its failures occurred during a time when walks required as many as nine balls, and bats could be flat on one side (shocking, literally). Whatever happened pre-1900 isn't particularly lauded or condemned today. It just . . . happened.

Very few people know much about Pud Galvin, Pittsburgh's best player of the era (1885–89, 1891–92), but the Hall of Famer turned out to be baseball's first 300-game winner (365 Ws). To be fair, probably very few know about baseball's first 300-game *loser* back then, either . . . Oh. Wait. Yeah, that's Pud Galvin, too (310 Ls). It was a wacky period.

To the franchise's credit, when the modern game *did* finally start to take shape, and the American League formed in 1901, launching the framework for the Major League Baseball we now know and love ... Pittsburgh immediately stepped up as the game's best.

Pittsburgh won its first two league titles in 1901–02, and played in the first World Series in 1903, falling to the Boston Americans in a best-of-nine (5–3). Hall of Fame shortstop Honus Wagner, unlike Galvin, propelled the Pirates at a time that history would remember fondly.

Wagner joined the club in 1900 and proceeded to lead the team in WAR every season until 1910 (8.3 average). He led the Buccos to their first World Series Championship in 1909, and laid the foundation for success that would stretch over several decades. The Pirates, while not regular champions, were seemingly always in the hunt.

In the modern era, the Pirates didn't have their 10th sub-.500 season until 1946. Meanwhile, their NL foe, Boston Braves, had reached their 10th sub-.500 campaign by 1911. Things always seemed to turn out well for Pittsburgh.

In 1960, bookended by two sub-80-win seasons, the Pirates came from nowhere to win the pennant (95–59), defeating the Yankees by way of Bill Mazeroski's famous Game 7-ending home run—the only walk-off in Game 7 history. Outfielder Roberto Clemente had his first All-Star season that year, and, much like Wagner a half-century prior, had ignited the charge for another long, successful, Buccos run.

The Pirates thrice won 90 games in the decade following the 1960 title, carrying momentum into the 1970s, when the Pirates excelled. From 1970–79, Pittsburgh played in the NLCS six times, winning the World Series twice (1971/79).

[Musical note: The Pirates' theme song that 1979 championship season was "We Are Family" by Sister Sledge, a Philadelphia group. By 1979, the Phillies were mired in a 96-year championship drought. Just thinking maybe Pittsburgh should have let Philly have that one.]

Since Pittsburgh's glorious '70s, things have been mostly rough for the club. They had Barry Bonds, but lost him before he became *BARRY BONDS*. Then they opened the beautiful PNC Park in 2001, but wasted its new-stadium smell, as the franchise was smack dab in the middle of a 20-year sub-.500 stretch of complete futility (1993–2012).

Andrew McCutchen is here to save the day. The Pirates have made the playoffs the last three seasons with the 2013 NL MVP leading the way. McCutchen looks like the two tide-turning captains that came before him, Wagner and Clemente, but he'll need some gold rings to cement his Pirates legacy.

The Flying Dutchman

The New Bill James Historical Baseball Abstract, a book by rock star baseball historian, Bill James, covers pretty much everything that ever happened in baseball history in incredible detail. And, in certain spots, it reads like a desperate plea to anoint Honus Wagner as one of the very best players to step into a batter's box.

Willie Mays, Ty Cobb, Ted Williams—all great players. But, according to James, when it comes to Wagner, only Babe Ruth was better. Who knew? Wagner is perhaps penalized for playing during baseball's unsexy Deadball Era, however.

Popularity aside, the Dutchman's stats back the claim:

- In National League history, ranks first in triples (252), and fourth in hits (3,420), doubles (643), and stolen bases (723).
- Won eight batting titles, tied with Tony Gwynn for the most in NL history.
- Was the only NL player during baseball's modern era to hit .325+ with 500+ stolen bases (.328, 629 SBs).
- Had twice as many seasons with 35+ doubles and 35+ stolen bases than any other player in baseball history (8)—as many as Ty Cobb (4), "Shoeless" Joe Jackson (2), and Vlad Guerrero (2), combined.

Wagner played before Babe Ruth broke all the rules and home run records. While it doesn't show in his career home run total (101), he was one of the game's elite power hitters when sluggers were primarily keeping balls inside the park.

The mug, and infamous schnoz of Honus Wagner; 1914. (Charles M. Conlon)

The Flying Dutchman led the league in slugging percentage eight times in his career, and was third in the National League in home runs during his Pirates career (82 HRs; 1900–17). Spanning baseball's modern era, Wagner is the only NL player with a .460+ slugging (.468 SLG) while hitting less than 100 home runs (minimum 4,000 plate appearances). And all this from a predominantly defensive position.

In baseball history, only two shortstops have led the league in every slash-line category (batting average/on-base percentage/

slugging)—both Pirates. Bucco Arky Vaughan was the last to do it in 1935 (.385/.491/.607), while Wagner did it THREE TIMES, in 1904 (.349/.423./.520), 1907 (.350/.408/.513), and 1908 (.354/.415/.542).

The Family

The Pirates won the NL East six times in the 1970s, culminating in a 1979 championship behind a galvanizing theme.

"The Family" was etched in the dugout roof, and first baseman Willie Stargell selected the popular disco hit "We Are Family" as the team's theme. The idea was mutually beneficial to the team, and song—national exposure of the single during the Pirates' playoff run helped Sister Sledge sell over a million copies of their album that year. For the Pirates, at least, the family was a long time in the making.

Roberto Clemente *(OF, 1955–72)*: There are plenty of icons in baseball history, and Clemente is one of the most revered. The 12-time Gold Glove outfielder, four-time batting champ, 3,000 hit club member, and 1966 MVP is, to this day, a hero in the Latin community. Sadly, he died in a plane crash in 1973 off the coast of Puerto Rico, on his way to Nicaragua, to help aid earthquake victims. He had finished his previous season with exactly 3,000 hits, but his legacy was about more than numbers.

The vocal black-Latino often said he felt doubly discriminated against, but the burden never showed. Baseball and life were two games Clemente had mastered. He played relentlessly, like his life depended on it, and died helping people whose lives were dependent on his charitable endeavors. The Hall of Fame honored him with enshrinement in 1973, making him one of just three players in baseball history to break the five-year waiting period (Babe Ruth, Lou Gehrig). His #21 jersey might some day join Jackie Robinson's #42 in universal MLB retirement.

But, about those numbers . . .

Clemente (94.5) is behind just Honus Wagner (120.3) in franchise career WAR. Oddly enough, the two each played exactly 2,433 games with Pittsburgh, with Clemente totaling just nine fewer plate appearances.

He had good speed, leading all of baseball in triples during his 18-year stretch in the bigs (166). Willie Mays was second, but 48 triples behind. Despite all those triples, Clemente only stole 83 career bases. Rickey Henderson had five *seasons* with more stolen bases than that, but had just 66 career triples. Clemente hit 85 triples just after his thirtieth birthday.

Nineteen seventy-three was a sudden passing of the torch, as newcomer Dave Parker was tasked with replacing a legend in right field, and Willie Stargell had to step up as the team's main attraction.

Dave Parker *(OF, 1973–83)*: "Cobra" started with a bang, batting .318 through his first six years in the big leagues. After his first four full seasons, he had two batting titles under his belt (1977–78), hitting .324 with a per 162-game average of 25 home runs and 109 RBIs.

From 1975–79, his best five-year stretch in a Pirates uniform, Parker led the league in batting average (.321) and triples (47), and was second in doubles (184) and extra-base hits (345).

Willie Stargell *(1B, 1962–82)*: A Hall of Fame slugger for 21 years with the Pirates, "Pops" had the respect and admiration of his peers and rivals. One of his notably epic homers at Philadelphia's Vet Stadium in 1971 hit the previously untouchable 600-level, and would be commemorated with a yellow star at its landing spot for over 30 years—and this was at the home of a cross-state rival! But, it was worthy. Teammate Richie Hebner, after venturing up to the landing spot, remarked, "It looked like a twenty-dollar cab ride from there to home plate."

Stargell's 475 home runs are the most in franchise history—296 of which led the majors during the 1970s. He's the only player in baseball history to win the MVP (1979), Roberto Clemente Award (Community; 1974), Babe Ruth Award (Postseason MVP; 1979), Lou Gehrig Memorial Award (Character; 1974), and the Hutch Award (Perseverance; 1978).

McClutch

These days, Andrew McCutchen has been the Pirates' biggest difference maker. In the 20 years from 1993 to 2012, Pittsburgh did not have a single season over .500, but, since McCutchen's first All-Star season in 2011, the team has averaged 86 wins per year.

Cutch was the only player in baseball to slash .300/.400/.500 each season from 2012–14, and he's the only player in baseball history with 200+ total bases, 50+ walks, and 15+ stolen bases in each of his first six seasons.

Andrew McCutchen, 2012. (Keith Allison, KeithAllisonPhoto.com)

In good company . . .

McCutchen and Barry Bonds are the only players with at least 40 extra-base hits, 50 walks, and 10 stolen bases in each of their first seven seasons.

McCutchen and Jackie Robinson are the only players with at least 200 total bases, 50 walks, and 10 stolen bases in each of their first seven seasons.

For three straight years, from 2012–14, McCutchen slashed at least .300/.400/.500 with 15+ stolen bases. Willie Mays only had three such seasons in his entire career. Cutch was the first Pirates player to pull off the consecutive feat since Honus Wagner back in 1903–05.

STATS INCREDIBLE!

1902: The 103–36 Pirates club, which never had a single losing streak longer than two games all season. Only team to accomplish this since 1901.

6: Times Ralph Kiner led the majors in home runs. Only Babe Ruth did it more times (11).

21: The height, in feet, of the right field wall at PNC Park, in honor of #21 Roberto Clemente.

38: The amount of games Barry Bonds had both a home run and a stolen base—a Pirates record. Barry also had 64 such games with the Giants, good for their franchise record. His 102 total are the most in baseball history.

2.60: Right-hander Gerrit Cole's ERA in 2015, the lowest qualified ERA for a Pirates pitcher in 30 years. Cole's 19-win total was the highest in 25 years.

14: Career stolen bases by shortstop Dick Groat (1952–67). Rickey Henderson had 1,392 more swipes than Groat. But Groat had one more career triple than Henderson (67 to 66).

10/30: Starling Marte (2013–14) became the first Pirate with 10+ home runs and 30+ stolen bases in consecutive seasons since Barry Bonds (1989–92).

26.9%: Percentage of all Pirates hits from 1927–29, from the bats of Paul and Lloyd Waner.

1,484: Pitches of at least 95 MPH thrown by Gerrit Cole in 2015—most in all of baseball. His 106 strikeouts on pitches of at least 95 MPH were also tops in MLB.

134: In 2015, Cole and Francisco Liriano became the first Pirates duo with at least 200 strikeouts each in the franchise's 134-year history.

5: On August 22–23, 1970, Roberto Clemente had consecutive five-hit games.

1958: After the 1958 season, Roberto Clemente opted not to play winter ball in Puerto Rico; instead, he enlisted in the United States Marine Corps Reserves. He served a six-month active duty commitment and was a part of the Marine Corps Reserves until September 1964.

ST. LOUIS CARDINALS

Est. 1882

Stan Musial is the only player in baseball history who ranks in the top 30 in singles (19th), doubles (third), triples (19th), and home runs (30th). He also ranks 13th all-time in bases on balls. He was able to do this despite giving up 15 months of his career to serve in the United States Navy during World War II. He was . . . The Man.

St. Louis has been called "Baseball Heaven," but let's get scientific . . . Two facts about the St. Louis Cardinals: They are the most successful team in National League history, and their fans are among the most respected and passionate in the game. What's tricky is determining which way to apply the cause and effect—the chicken (Cardinals) or the egg (fans)? Or maybe, correlation does not imply causation, and the success and support that the franchise has had are just two independently dynamite properties, like barley and hops, that have come together to create one truly special brew . . .

Meh. Who cares?

The mid-market Cardinals—fourth in all-time wins (10,571) with an NL-best 11 championships—are a true American success story any way you look at it.

Looking like the set of an Old Spice commercial, the team photo of the 1876 St. Louis Brown Stockings–the charter NL club which was the forerunner to today's St. Louis Cardinals franchise. (Author unknown; PD)

The Cards (then the Browns), had good genes from the start. They began their run of success in the 1880s, as part of the American Association, winning four straight league titles (1885–88) behind the tutelage of young skipper Charles Comiskey, a natural-born winner.

Comiskey's successful stint with the Browns (1885–89, 1891) was his first in a series of pivotally fortuitous ventures that would eventually lead him to establishing both the Chicago White Sox, and the American League as a whole, in the twentieth century. Just a footnote in the Cards' long, storied history, but Comiskey and the team's early triumphs were tremendously important. The one-and-done Seattle Pilots (Brewers), the original Baltimore Orioles (Yankees), and the Kansas City version of the Athletics could attest to the importance of early success on franchise staying power.

After the Cards/Browns joined the National League in 1892, they hit a bump in the road, finishing over .500 just four times over a 24-year span. A long time, for sure, but since infielder Rogers Hornsby arrived in 1917, the Cardinals, to date, have not had a single sub-.500 stretch that's lasted longer than three seasons.

Hornsby was an all-time great in the game's history, leading the Cardinals in WAR for ten straight seasons, before guiding the club to its first championship in 1926—interestingly, his last year with St. Louis and first year as player-manager. He was the first in a long string of superstars to pass through the Gateway to the West.

Hall of Famers Grover Cleveland Alexander, Jim Bottomley, Dizzy Dean, Johnny Mize, and Stan Musial all played pivotal roles in helping St. Louis reach nine World Series in 21 years from 1926–46, winning six (1926, 1931, 1934, 1942, 1944, 1946). Then, two literal game-changers in Bob Gibson and Curt Flood highlighted two more championship squads in 1964 and 1967.

Since, the Cardinals have just kept on winning, with a variety of styles. They won three NL titles and one ring with the game's best all-time defender (Ozzie Smith), and they won two World Series in three tries with one of the game's most dominant batsmen (Albert Pujols). Throughout the team's history, it's probably had the greatest collection of hitters, and has been incredibly consistent with rebuilding talent, year after year.

The Cardinals have had 22 All-Star nods the past four years, spread between 15 different players. St. Louis always finds players to deliver, and the fans do their part, helping the Cards finish in the top-four in NL attendance 19 of the past 20 seasons.

It's a match made in heaven.

The Bats

Rogers Hornsby *(2B, 1915–26)*: Not much is known about his childhood, but his mom named him "Rogers" after her maiden name, so we're pretty sure it was a weird situation. He developed into a notoriously difficult personality in baseball, especially during his 15 years managing. Jimmy Dugan, of Penny Marshall's Rockford Peaches, once said, "Rogers Hornsby was my manager, and he called me a talking pile of pigsh-t. And that was when my parents drove all the way down from Michigan to see me play the game. And did I cry?" No. He didn't. Because there's no crying in baseball. But opposing pitchers might have wanted to, after seeing Hornsby step into the batter's box.

Hornsby owns the top five seasons in Cardinals modern era history (post-1900) in terms of batting average, and thrice batted over .400 with the team in the 1920s. Consider—there have been just 13 .400+ batting average seasons in modern baseball history, and Hornsby hit .402 *OVER A FIVE-YEAR STRETCH,* from 1921–25. During a ridiculous 762-game stretch, from September 9, 1920 to May 30, 1926, he maintained an even .400.

Hornsby ranks first all-time in on-base percentage by a right-handed batter (.434), and is 20 points ahead of any other primary second baseman in career batting average (.358). In the 1,106 wins Hornsby was a part of during his 23-year career, he batted .406/.484/.672. Hornsby even batted .312/.383/.484 in losses, comparable to Hall of Famer Billy Dickey's overall career slash line of .313/.384/.486.

In what is surely a feather in his cap, Hornsby's methods served as inspiration to the great Ted Williams, the only player during the Live Ball Era to top Hornsby's single-season batting average above MLB average (.1433 to .1371; 1941, 1924, respectively).

Stan Musial *(OF, 1941–44, 1946–63)*: A contemporary of Ted Williams, Musial is one of the most comparable to the Splendid Splinter. A quick look at Musial's 22-year Cards career—three-time NL MVP, 20-time All-Star, .331 career hitter—and it's easy to see why he was "The Man" in St. Louis.

Musial was productive from start to finish. From his very first game until his very last, his career batting average never dipped below .319. He won two MVPs, three World Series, and a World War (serving in the US Navy in 1945) before the age of twenty-six. In his final full season, in 1962, at the age of forty-one, Musial hit .330, a league record for quadragenarians.

When he retired in 1963, Musial held National League records for hits (3,630), extra-base hits (1,377), and RBIs (1,951). He was baseball's first 400-homer, 3,000-hit player, and the NL's only 200-homer, 3,000-hit, .400+ on-base percentage player.

Musial was an extra-base hit king of the modern era (third all-time), and distributed them evenly, mashing 475 home runs, but also finishing in the top-10 in career doubles (third, 725) and triples (10th, 177). Since 1920, there have been just nine seasons in which a player hit 40+ doubles and 20+ triples. Musial is the only one to do it twice (1943, 1946).

Over a six-year stretch, from 1943–49, Musial batted .350, averaging 211 hits and 44 doubles per season. Hall of Famer Willie Mays never had a *single season* with either a batting average, hits total, or doubles total that high.

Mark McGwire *(1B, 1997–2001)*: A poster boy for the steroid era, McGwire will have a very difficult time making it into the Hall of Fame. However, because it's impossible to know exactly who else may have been using performance-enhancing drugs at the time, it's hard to penalize the guy too much. After all, when (supposedly) clean, this was the same guy who clobbered the rookie home run record with 49 bombs for Oakland in 1987. His freakish power came naturally, even if his freakish numbers with St. Louis may have been aided.

McGwire's time in St. Louis was all about breaking Roger Maris's single-season home run record (61 HR), and Mac reached that goal, clobbering the 37-year-old record with 70 homers in

1998. Actually, during his five seasons in St. Louis overall, he averaged 65 home runs per 162 games. While the 1998 home run race with Sammy Sosa (66 HRs) was thrilling, McGwire's breaking it was inevitable, and only a matter of whether he'd be able to play a full season.

McGwire struggled to stay healthy throughout his career, and his home run total reflects this. Despite being tops in baseball history in home run percentage (7.61%) and at-bats per home run (1 per every 10.6 at-bats), his 583 jacks are just 10th on the all-time list. If Barry Bonds had went deep at the same rate as McGwire, he would have finished his career with a mind-boggling 959 home runs.

Still, McGwire's 135 two-year home run total while with the Cards in 1998–99 is still tops in baseball history. He broke down and was unable to play 100 games in either of his final two seasons (2000–01), but he was still valuable. Over the final 162 games played in his career, McGwire had 49 home runs and 103 walks.

Albert Pujols *(1B, 2001–11)*: Pronounced *POO-holes,* Prince Albert's got a name that'll make you snicker, with a game more powerful than a Dick Butkus open-field tackle . . . Bat speed quicker than Dick Trickle's #84 Buick on a straightaway . . . You get the idea.

While his four seasons in Los Angeles (2012–15) have been rather pedestrian (.266/.326/.478, 29 HRs per), his first 11 while with St. Louis were historic, yet familiar.

Pujols's .328/.420/.617 slash line with St. Louis is very similar to the .331/.417/.559 posted by Stan Musial over twice as many seasons. In terms of run production, however, Pujols was well ahead of Musial, averaging 28 more runs scored per season (117 to 89) with 32 more RBIs (121 to 89). Of course, it's unfair to compare the two, not just because of generational differences, but because this was Pujols's best stretch of his entire career—not his career as a whole.

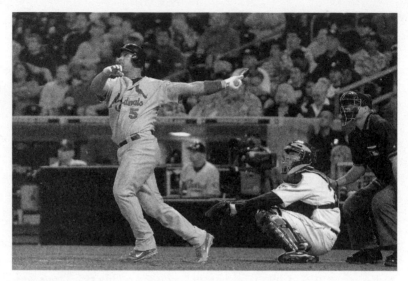

Albert Pujols homering at Petco Park in 2008—the last season anyone hit .357/.462/.653 or better. (Dirk Hansen, CC BY-SA 3.0)

However, even if we compare, apples-to-apples, just their first 11 full seasons, Pujols still leads in nearly every offensive category, though Musial (.345/.432/.582) draws to about as close to Pujols as physically possible.

That's how good he was (is?)—better than *The Man*.

Pujols was also better than probably everyone in the 2000s, collecting a rare decade-Triple Crown, leading the National League in batting average (.334), home runs (366), and RBIs (1,112) from 2000–09.

The Arms

No offense to Cardinals pitchers, but, historically, this franchise has been defined by its offense. That being said, two pitchers surely stand out amongst the rest.

Dizzy Dean *(1930, 1932–37)*: It's generally thought that Jay Dean's nickname was a playful knock on his colorful, dimwitted demeanor. On the mound, however, the right-hander was serious, and one of the most talented pitchers in the game's history.

Injuries cut Dean's career to just six full seasons (1932–37), but the Hall of Famer made a major impact in that time, winning an MVP in 1934, finishing runner-up the next two seasons, and ranking #85 on *The Sporting News's* top-100 players list, compiled in 1999.

Dean was the last National League pitcher to win 30 games in a season (1934; 30–7, 2.66 ERA), and he nearly did it twice, winning 28 the following year. Only six pitchers in the NL have won 26+ games in a season since Dean *averaged* a 27–12 record over *four* seasons, from 1934–36.

Bob Gibson *(1959–75)*: A lifetime Cardinal, Gibson was one of the most dominant pitchers to ever live.

Taken as a whole, his career was impressive—251 wins, 2.91 ERA, 3,117 strikeouts—but he's most famous for his lights-out 1968 campaign.

That year, Gibson was 22–9, with a microscopic 1.12 ERA, winning both the NL Cy Young award and MVP. The only players with lower single-season ERAs were Dutch Leonard (0.96; 1914) and Mordecai Brown (1.04; 1906), during a time when yearly college tuition was about $150, stop signs were a new thing, and people had awesome names like "Dutch" and "Mordecai."

Of his 22 wins that year, 13 were shutouts—which was more than his home runs and triples allowed, combined (11).

Heck, even his ERA in his nine *losses* (2.24) would have qualified for the sixth-best NL ERA mark overall.

Gibson's historic year is often credited as the main culprit for the mound being lowered the following year, in 1969. Game-changer.

In the postseason, Gibson was just as dominant, posting a 7–2 record, 1.89 ERA, and 0.883 WHIP during 81 World Series innings (earned a ring in 1964 and 1967). He is the National League's World Series leader in wins (7) and strikeouts (91).

[Then & Now: Clayton Kershaw might be the best equivalent to Gibson today, but it's a difficult comparison. Kershaw has 21 complete games to date, while Gibson had 19 just in games that went extra innings.]

The Glove

Ozzie Smith *(SS, 1982–96)*, the Wizard, batted just .262 in his career—the eighth-lowest batting average among Hall of Fame position players (5,000 at-bat minimum). But, the 15-time All-Star may have been the best defensive player in the game's history.

Not surprisingly, Smith ranks best all-time in defensive WAR (43.4). Sure, he would have to return to baseball and collect 531 straight hits for his average to creep above .300, but, in terms of total WAR, Ozzie actually ranks ahead of the great Derek Jeter, 76.5 to 71.8. Jeter hit .310 in his career, but the Wizard had a whopping 485 more defensive runs saved than the Captain (238.7 to -246.3).

STATS INCREDIBLE!

68: The total amount of home runs hit by the entire Cardinals team in 1991—two fewer than Mark McGwire hit for St. Louis in 1998.

6: The number of MLB seasons in which a player had 20+ home runs and more homers than singles. McGwire owns five of them. From 1994 to 2001, he had 354 home runs to just 353 singles.

0.98: Bob Gibson's ERA over a 34-game stretch, from September 12, 1967 to September 6, 1968.

.216: Opponents' batting average against Gibson from 1965–70. Gibson batted .224 himself over that span.

16: Johnny Mize's total triples in 1938—the most in MLB history by a player with no stolen bases. Mize's 14 triples the following Cards season is the second-most by a player with no stolen bases.

6: Tied with the Cubs' Sammy Sosa, Mize had the most career 3-homer games in history.

7: Lou Brock's record for stolen bases in a single World Series. He did it twice, in 1967 and 1968—including three swipes in Game 7 of the 1967 World Series.

289: Minor league games played by Randy Poffo—a.k.a. pro wrestler "Macho Man Randy Savage." He slashed .282/.400/.441 in 1973, his final season in the Cardinals organization.

1st: Pitcher Mitchell Harris debuted on April 25, 2015 for the Cards, the first US Naval Academy graduate to play in the majors since Cpt. Willard "Nemo" Gaines on July 16, 1921.

21: Postseason games won by the Cards since Pujols signed with the Angels at the end of 2011. The Angels have won *none.*

3,630: Career hits by Stan Musial—1,815 at home and 1,815 on the road.

NATIONAL LEAGUE WEST

ARIZONA DIAMONDBACKS

Est. 1998

In 2012, Paul Goldschmidt had 43 doubles, 20 home runs, and 18 stolen bases—becoming the youngest first baseman with 40+ doubles, 20+ homers, and 10+ steals since Lou Gehrig in 1927.

In 1998, the Arizona Diamondbacks were a new, expansion franchise. In 2001, they won the World Series. What took the Philadelphia Phillies 97 years to accomplish, the D-Backs did in four. FOUR.

It's the fastest championship for a new franchise in the game's history, but it wasn't just beginner's luck. Arizona targeted talented, undervalued veterans—Steve Finley, Luis Gonzalez, Randy Johnson, Curt Schilling, and others—at a time when most new franchises' best hopes would still be hacking away in Triple-A. At the turn of the century, everything the Diamondbacks touched turned to gold . . .

1999:
- SS Jay Bell, age thirty-three, had a career high in homers (38) his second season with Arizona.

- 3B Matt Williams, thirty-three, also in his second Arizona season, became one of just five third basemen in baseball history to knock in over 140 runs (142 RBIs).
- OF Gonzalez, thirty-one, during his first season with the team, hit then career highs in hits (206), batting average (.336), home runs (26), and RBIs (111).
- OF Finley, thirty-four, another newbie, put up the most home runs (34) and RBIs (103) of his career.
- SP Johnson, thirty-five, was a steal in free agency, hitting career highs in innings pitched (271.2), complete games (12), and strikeouts (364), en route to his first of four straight Cy Young Awards.

2001:
- SP Schilling, thirty-four, recorded his first 20-win season (22 Ws) in his first full year with the D-Backs.
- OF Reggie Sanders, thirty-three, had the highest home run total of his career (33)—his first and only season with the club.
- SP/RP Miguel Batista, thirty, a new Diamondback, soared to new personal highs in wins (11) and ERA (3.36).

Arizona defeated the New York Yankees in a thrilling 2001 World Series, and did it without a single starting position player in their twenties. It would have been logical to assume that the Diamondbacks would be in for a swift decline thereafter, but it has been a remarkably consistent franchise ever since.

In its 18 years as an MLB club, the Diamondbacks have never had a three-year stretch without at least one second-place finish, or higher. After two straight sub-.500 performances through 2014–15, Arizona will be looking to make a signature surge in 2016.

The Big(ger) Unit

The Big Unit, Randy Johnson, was, at times, the best pitcher in baseball while with Seattle (1989–98). His six-year stretch with Arizona, however, put him in the discussion as one of the greatest power pitchers in the game's history.

Johnson, the team's career WAR leader (53), also holds the franchise Triple Crown, leading the Diamondbacks all-time in wins (118), ERA (2.83), and strikeouts (2,077). He shares the MLB record for consecutive Cy Young awards (4; 1999–02) and is the lone Diamondbacks representative in the Baseball Hall of Fame.

With an upper-90s fastball to match his six-foot-ten frame and menacing scowl, Johnson was the perfect strikeout machine (or potential movie villain).

In 2001, he struck out 372 batters, nearly topping Nolan Ryan's modern era mark of 383 set in 1973, despite pitching more than 75 innings less than Ryan (249.2 to 326). Taking a 325-inning stretch from July 9, 2000 to September 2, 2001, Johnson amassed a super-human 488 strikeouts. And he was still deadly accurate with his pitches.

Ryan led the league in walks the year he set the record (162 BBs), while Johnson, surrendering just 71 walks in 2001, joined Sandy Koufax (1965; 382 Ks, 71 BBs) as the only two players to have 300 more strikeouts than walks since Matt Kilroy in 1886 (513 Ks, 182 BBs) . . . when seven balls were required for a walk.

Over the course of Johnson's career, and especially while with Arizona, left-handed batters didn't stand much of a chance. Southpaw legend Steve Carlton, a pitcher, had a higher batting average during his career (.201) than the 22 years' worth of left-handed batters to face Johnson (.199). During his 1999 campaign in which he led the league in batters faced, lefties, incredibly, hit just .103 against him, collecting 11 total bases. Twenty-three MLB batters in 2015 alone collected 11 total bases in one single game.

When Curt Schilling was added to the mix in 2000, things got a little unfair for the opposition.

Acey Deucey

Johnson and Schilling finished 1–2 in the Cy Young voting their first two full seasons playing together. They combined for 43 wins in 2001 and set a new, two-teammate, modern era record for strikeouts, with 665.

The duo combined for a 19.6 WAR in 2002, the best season total for any two rotation mates of the Live Ball Era.

Their record over both seasons was 90–24, a .789 win percentage. Over the past 13 seasons, no SINGLE pitcher has had consecutive seasons with a win percentage that high.

Schill didn't get the Cy Young hardware because of his All-World teammate, but he deserves *something* for being, arguably, the most efficient power pitcher in history. In 2001, beyond just leading the league in wins (22), Schilling became one of just two players in MLB history (Pedro Martinez, 1999) with 290+ strikeouts and less than 40 walks in the same season—and in 2002, he did it again.

Curt Schilling and Randy Johnson shared World Series MVP honors in 2001. (AP Photo/Elaine Thompson)

Luckily, there was one piece of hardware that Schilling could at least share with Johnson in 2001—World Series MVP. It's the only instance the award has ever been split, and they were worthy recipients.

The Unit was 3–0 with a microscopic 1.04 ERA in the Series, and Schilling wasn't far behind, going 1–0 with a 1.69. Overall, Johnson was 5–1, with a 1.52 ERA in 41.1 postseason innings in 2001, while Schilling finished at 4–0, with a 1.12 ERA in 48.1 innings. Schilling pitched the most innings of anyone in history with a perfect postseason record. Not surprisingly, the two sit 1–2 on the single postseason wins list among starting pitchers.

The Other Half

The story of the D-backs success goes beyond the pitching mound.

The team was loaded, top to bottom, in 2001, so it's unfair to credit just the offense or just the pitching. As a team, Arizona finished with the fourth-best batting average in the NL (.267), scoring the third-most runs (818). Luis Gonzalez had one of the greatest seasons in league history, finishing third in MVP voting behind Barry Bonds and Sammy Sosa. That was the season Bonds broke the single season home run record (73 HRs), so even if MVP voting was exclusive to Gonzalez's blood relatives and D. Baxter the Bobcat, it was still Bonds's trophy to lose.

Gonzalez (.325/57 HRs/142 RBIs) and Sosa (.328/64/160) were the first players since 1938 to register a .325+/50+/140+ season. Gonzo slugged .688 that season playing in the full 162 games, which is the highest slugging percentage ever for a player appearing in all 162.

The plan to acquire talented veterans like Gonzalez paid dividends very early for Arizona—the 1999 squad is the only team in history to have four players with over 74 extra-base hits (Gonzalez, Jay Bell, Steve Finley, Matt Williams)—which also led to a relatively short window for contention.

Jay Bell, who in 1999 (38 HRs) was just the fifth second baseman with a 38+ homer season, was done as an everyday player by 2002.

Steve Finley, still going strong in 2003, was the first player in franchise history to hit double digits in home runs (22), triples (10), and stolen bases (15) in the same season, and Stephen Drew in 2010 is the only D-back to match the feat. Finley's last season in Arizona came in 2004, at age thirty-nine.

The young franchise was heavy with older talent, and eventually time caught up with some of Arizona's top veterans. The Diamondbacks have only made the playoffs twice in the last 13 seasons, but first baseman Paul Goldschmidt (8.8 WAR, fifth in MLB in 2015) could help spark another championship run.

Goldy won the stat-geek Triple Crown in 2013, leading the NL in OPS+ (160), home runs (36), and RBIs (125). He became just the seventh first baseman in MLB history with 35+ doubles, 35+ homers, and 15+ steals in the same season.

STATS INCREDIBLE!

9: The number of seasons Randy Johnson had more strikeouts than baserunners allowed. No other pitcher has had five such seasons.

7/20: Randy Johnson had enough strikeouts on July 20th of both 1999 and 2000 to lead the league in strikeouts for each season.

275: Johnson and Curt Schilling, in 2001, became the first duo with 275+ strikeouts each since Tim Keefe and Jack Lynch in 1884. They repeated the feat in 2002.

19.6: Combined WAR of Johnson and Schilling in 2002. Highest season WAR total for a 1–2 during the Live Ball Era (post-1919).

.185: The total batting average of opponents that fell behind 0–1 in the count to Johnson. They batted .232 when he fell behind 1–0. Just trying at all was hardly worth their effort . . .

9: Curt Schilling is the only pitcher in baseball history with a 9.00+ K/9 and 9.00+ K/BB in the same season (2002).

40: Johnson's age (plus 251 days) on May 18, 2004, making him the oldest pitcher to toss a perfect game.

488: In 1973, Nolan Ryan had a modern-record 383 strikeouts in 326 innings. From July 9, 2000 to September 2, 2001, Randy Johnson had 488 strikeouts in 325 innings.

.321: Paul Goldschmidt's batting average in 2015, with 33 home runs and 21 stolen bases. He was the second first baseman ever to bat .320 or better in a season with at least 20 home runs and 20 stolen bases (Carl Yastrzemski, 1970).

142: Brandon Webb had a career 142 ERA+, besting Johan Santana (136), Randy Johnson (135), Greg Maddux (132), Sandy Koufax (131), and Roy Halladay (131).

COLORADO ROCKIES

Est. 1993

Todd Helton batted .345/.441/.607 at Coors Field and .287/.386/.469 everywhere else. Hall of Famer Chuck Klein batted .395/.448/.705 at the Baker Bowl and .277/.339/.451 everywhere else.

When things don't happen for a while, it's natural to stubbornly think they *can't* happen. Like thinking a team can't win a championship. The Cubs are currently in a 107-year championship drought, and I'm sure there are tons of Chicago fans who have accepted the team's sorry fate as cosmic certainty. But that's just superstitious pessimism. With the Rockies, it's oddly scientific.

Playing at Coors Field, almost exactly a mile above sea level (5,200 feet), Denver's Colorado Rockies entered the league in 1993 amid a cloud of skepticism in regards to fair playing conditions. The thin, dry air, it is said, creates a climate for (literally) heightened offensive play, making the balls harder and their carry higher and longer. But, as noted in the film, *Jurassic Park*—an early name proposal for Coors Field—*life finds a way*.

Stadium designers pushed back the fences at the onset, and the team later installed humidors to control the condition of baseballs put in play. Of course, deeper fences create spacious outfields, ripe for singles and doubles hitters to pick apart, and humidors do nothing to solve the thin-air problem. Coors Field, and the Rockies franchise itself, is thus a conundrum of both man and nature pushing back at one another. As such, if one were to make a case that the Rockies *can't* win a championship, they could certainly *Bill Nye*–up a PowerPoint presentation that makes a viable case—at least, more functionally than that of some cosmic vendetta against Colorado baseball.

The truth is, Colorado's environment may narrowly impede its chances at winning a championship, but it does not prevent it from pulling it off. If the backdrop is an opponent, it's battled equally by both home and away teams. Sure, even lately, Coors Field has been the highest-scoring stadium in baseball six of the past seven years, and that makes for tough contract negotiations with free agent pitchers. But, the teams that win championships often do so because they make difficult propositions—like wading through thin free agent pools, or finding stars in the draft's later rounds—fruitful. And Colorado has had its chances.

The Rockies made their lone World Series appearance in 2007, after winning 21 of their final 22 contests (14–1 to end the regular season, 7–0 in the playoffs entering the World Series). Beginning that season, they had a four-year stretch averaging 85 wins per year. Not phenomenal, but still proof that sustained success is possible in Colorado, even if the team's biggest names, historically, have been on the offensive side.

Over the years, Rockies superstars like Larry Walker, Todd Helton, and Troy Tulowitzki have lit up the scoreboard and made the game exciting in a city that has (minor league) baseball roots dating back to the 1880s. Denver is a great baseball town, and the game there has always been exciting. Their 1993 expansion mate, the Miami Marlins, may have a pair of titles in hand, but the two clubs share the exact same 162-game average record (76–86). And Colorado has the stronger fan base, routinely finishing in or near the top half in NL attendance.

Troy Tulowitzki's final home game at Colorado's cavernous Coors Field; July 25, 2015. (Flickr TheLastCanadian, CC BY-SA)

Inevitably, scientifically, indubitably, this team will win a championship. And at the rate they score, it's sure to be one of the most exciting runs in baseball history.

So Offensive

Twenty-three years in, the Denver effect has proven to be undeniably real. Their very first season in 1993, the Rockies finished third in the National League in OPS (.745), higher than the San Diego Padres have ever ranked in their 47-year history. The Rockies have led the league in batting average more times (12) than the Braves (9)—the oldest continually operating team in baseball, dating back to 1871. During an eight-year stretch, from 1995 to 2002, the Rockies finished first in the NL in batting average, aided by the franchise-leading bats of Larry Walker and Todd Helton. Of course, the Coors Field "beer goggles" tend to paint a prettier picture of the two sluggers' careers.

(Ryan Fitzpatrick)

Larry Walker *(OF, 1995–2005)*: Walker signed with Colorado after six seasons with Montreal, and immediately hit career-highs in home runs (36) and RBIs (101). He's the franchise leader in batting average (.334), and no one in baseball has had more .350+ batting average seasons (4) than Walker over the last 25 years.

Over 10 seasons, Walker won three batting titles, an MVP award, and five Gold Gloves. In 1997, batting .366 with 49 home runs and 33 stolen bases, he became the only .350/30/30 man in the game's history.

So. Lock for the Hall of Fame, right? Not so fast . . .

Walker's .313 career batting average is tempered by the fact that he batted .381 at Coors. He put up astounding 162-game averages of 41 home runs and 141 RBIs at home, and the numbers get even crazier when broken down per season.

Walker led the league with a .379 average in 1999, but, in 232 at-bats at home that year, he batted an other-worldly .461. If he had played a full 162-game season, maintaining his Coors Field stats at home and on the road, he would have established new single-season records for batting average, home runs (63), hits (262), and total bases (.500). Instead, he batted just .286 on the road, with an extra-base hit total (24) that was less than his home-park home run total alone that season (26).

Walker was an all-around star who played exceptionally in the field and the batter's box, particularly at home. But, with a career road slash line of .278/.370/.495, Cooperstown may not be as welcoming as Denver, Colorado.

Todd Helton *(1B, 1997–2013)*: Helton's career numbers (.316/.414/.539) are eerily similar to Walker's (.313/.400/.565), but Helton spent his entire 17-year career in Colorado, putting his name atop most of the franchise's offensive categories.

His 2000 season was monstrous, as he led the league in hits (216), doubles (59), RBIs (147), and entire slash line (.372/.463/.698). He became the first player since 1932 with 100+ singles, 100+ extra-base hits, and 100+ walks in the same season. With 25 multi-extra-base hit games, Helton tied Lou Gehrig (1934) and Babe Ruth (1921) for the most in a single year. Of the 15 seasons in MLB history of 100+ extra-base hits, Helton is the only one to pull it off in consecutive seasons (2000, 2001). Also during 2000–01, Helton became the game's first and only player to have multiple seasons with 50+ doubles and 40+ homers. His two-year consecutive doubles total (113) is the second-highest in modern baseball history (120; Joe Medwick, 1936–37).

To pile on unnecessarily—Helton (5), Jeff Bagwell, and Albert Pujols (6) are the only first basemen in NL history with five or more seasons of a 1.000+ OPS. He was super good.

So. Lock for the Hall of Fame, right? Well . . .

Like in Walker's case, though not as extreme, Coors Field was kind to Helton. He batted .345/.441/.607 at home over his career, compared to just .287/.386/.469 on the road. He hit 369 home runs overall, but his 162-game road average was just 20, compared to 32 at the Mile High confines. So, it's reasonable to suggest, with everything being equal, Helton was a very good player, but not necessarily one of the best of his generation, as his career numbers might superficially indicate.

Still, Helton *feels* like he will eventually be Colorado's first representative in Cooperstown. He's had more doubles (592) than any first baseman in history, and only 54% of his two-baggers came via the spacious Coors outfield. And if he does pull it off, Walker, provided he remains on the ballot, might then find his road to enshrinement a tad smoother.

Getting Defensive

Colorado trailed in the NL West by as many as seven games in September of 2007, and trailed the Wild Card by 4.5 with 14 games remaining in the regular season. The team went 13–1 during that final stretch, forcing a one-game playoff with San Diego. After winning the play-in game with the Padres, they swept the Phillies in the opening round (3–0), then swept the Diamondbacks to take the NLCS crown (4–0). They wound up on the wrong side of a sweep to the Red Sox in the World Series (0–4), but it's almost a side note to the incredible 21–1 stretch that got them there.

The Rockies tied a National League record for most consecutive wins to start a postseason (7), and tied another NL record for most consecutive wins during a combined regular season and postseason stretch (10). The Rockies were showing how dominant they could be with competitive pitching.

Only twice in franchise history have the Rockies finished higher than 12th in the league in ERA. Both times (eighth; 2007, 2009), they made the postseason—the only two playoff bids in the club's 23-year run. From 2007–10, Colorado fielded the best pitching staff in its history.

The Rockies' top four hurlers in career pitching WAR all shared a rotation for Colorado in 2010—the only team in the league whose top four pitched together. Of course, this speaks more to their historically dreadful showing on the mound, but the team certainly had significant talent.

Right-hander Ubaldo Jimenez, it could be said, was the first true ace for Colorado. He's the team's career leader in ERA (3.66), WHIP (1.284), and K/9 (8.175). His 2010 performance was the best in club history, by far.

Jimenez set new franchise bests for wins (19), WHIP (1.155), and strikeouts (214). He pitched the lowest ERA in team history (2.88), and he's the only Rockie ever—EVER—to register a sub-3.00 ERA with at least 115 innings pitched. By comparison, just in 2015, the St. Louis Cardinals' top five starters combined for a 2.92 ERA.

Despite playing at Coors Field (have we mentioned it's a hitters park?), he didn't allow a single home run to any of the 408 batters to whom he pitched a first-pitch strike. At season's end, he had actually given up more homers on the road (6) than at home (4).

STATS INCREDIBLE!

40/40/30: In 1996, Rockies outfielder Ellis Burks became the game's first player with 40+ doubles, 40+ home runs, and 30+ steals ... In 1997, teammate Larry Walker became the second.

.986: Former Rockie Troy Tulowitzki's career fielding percentage, the best in baseball history at the shortstop position. He has yet to commit an error since his midseason trade to Toronto in 2015.

2: Number of Pro Bowl quarterbacks drafted by the Rockies—Michael Vick (887th overall) in 2000, and Russell Wilson (140th overall) in 2010.

105: Todd Helton's extra-base hit total in 2001, the most in the National League since Chuck Klein hit 107 for the Phillies in 1930.

.430: Larry Walker's batting average in 1999 after taking a first-pitch ball.

.397: Walker's batting average over a 179-game stretch, from July 19, 1998 to September 19, 1999.

LOS ANGELES DODGERS

Est. 1883

Don Newcombe served in both the US Army and the US Navy. He won both an MVP Award and a Cy Young Award. He is the only player in baseball history who is a US military veteran to win both an MVP Award and a Cy Young Award.

They went by several different names before landing on "Dodgers" in their original home, Brooklyn, NYC.

Along with Bridegrooms, the club took turns as the Atlantics, Grays, Grooms, Superbas, and Robins—without much success, before "Dodgers" became the permanent moniker in 1932. Actually, it wasn't until 1955 that Brooklyn would win its first championship, after coming up short in its seven previous trips to the World Series post-1900. The difference? More than any alteration in nickname or playing strategy, Brooklyn embraced social change more than any club in baseball history.

The most heralded fact attributed to the Dodgers is being the first major-league team in the modern era to sign an African American player—second baseman Jackie Robinson. The "modern era" qualifier in no way diminishes Robinson's heroically trailblazing accomplishments, but it is true that Robinson was, at best, MLB's fourth black player.

The first credited black player is generally considered to be William Edward White, who subbed into one game in 1879. This was only uncovered within the past decade, though, as White, for most of his life, identified *as white*. Brothers Fleetwood and Welday Walker came five years later, playing a combined 47 games for the Toledo Blue Stockings of the American Association in 1884. Racist influence forced the Walkers from the major-league game almost as quickly as they arrived, and not a single black player would don an MLB uniform until Robinson stood his ground in 1947.

Robinson is justly credited with handling the transition with tremendous courage, but the color-barrier incinerator did so much more. From the very beginning, in the face of tumultuous opposition, Robinson was one of the game's best second basemen, all-time.

He won the Rookie of the Year award in 1947, a league MVP two years later, and was the Dodgers' best player over the course of his career (1947–56), a 10-year stretch in which the team won an average of 95 games, reaching six World Series and winning one. Still, over the same period, the Dodgers were averaging just over 17,000 fans per game.

Dodgers owner Walter O'Malley moved the team to Los Angeles and set new attendance records each of the first three years on the West Coast (per game averages: 23,968; 26,552; 29,271), winning championships in 1959, 1963, and 1965. Really, ever since the move, the Dodgers have been one of the most consistently competitive franchises in baseball, never going longer than seven seasons out west without reaching the postseason.

Some of the best players in baseball history have donned the Dodger Blue uniform, extending the team's proud legacy, and

Fans sit outside the right field wall of Brooklyn's Ebbets Field in 1920.
(Bain News Service (LOC))

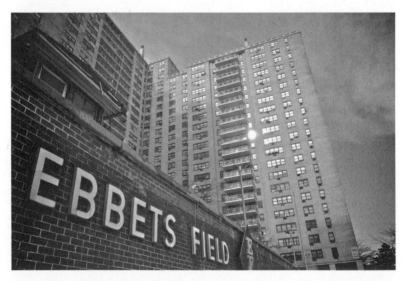

Same spot nearly 100 years later, the east-end wall of Brooklyn's Ebbets Field Apartments. (Saundi Wilson)

furthering the game's development. After 132 years and counting, though, one player has clearly worn it best.

Jackie Robinson

Breaking the color barrier and sticking with a major-league ball club is a great accomplishment in itself. To play at a Hall of Fame level, mostly over the age of thirty, while enduring historical scrutiny, is remarkable. It oozes respect.

Robinson came out of the gate strong, winning the Rookie of the Year in 1947, and receiving MVP votes each of his first seven seasons. He's one of two players all time (Andrew McCutchen) with 200 total bases, 50+ walks, and 10+ stolen bases in each of his first six seasons. He's one of just seven players in the modern era, and the only second baseman, with 170+ hits in each of his first five seasons. One season, specifically, Robinson had a truly special, all-time great performance.

In 1949, Robinson won the NL MVP and had one of the finest seasons ever for a second baseman. He batted .347 with 66 extra-base hits and 37 stolen bases. No player has had a .340+/65+ XBH/35+ SB season since. Not only was this the last instance of a player leading the NL in batting average and stolen bases, but 38 of his hits came with runners in scoring position—the most in recorded history. That clutch instinct gave Robinson by far the highest single-season RBI total of his career (124), making him just the third second baseman in NL history to reach the mark.

An on-base machine in 1949 (.432 OBP, second in NL), Robinson was second in the league in hits (203) and seventh in walks (86). He's the last second baseman in baseball with a 200/80 season.

Jackie Robinson, 1945, with the Kansas City Monarchs of the Negro Leagues, two seasons before his major-league call. (The Call Kansas City, 1945.0)

To this day, despite playing just 10 MLB seasons, Robinson ranks third all-time in total WAR for the Dodgers (61.5), and his 7.22 WAR per-162 games is the best in team history.

Oh yeah, and no one is allowed to wear his no. 42 jersey, ever (except on April 15, each season, when EVERYONE dons the "42" in his honor). *RESPECT.*

Shadow Warriors

Jackie Robinson casts a very big shadow in baseball history. He was a vital part of Brooklyn's success in the '40s and '50s, but a few Dodgers all-time greats played right alongside him.

Pee Wee Reese *(SS, 1940–58)*: Reese was the captain of multiple Dodgers generations, playing 16 seasons (missing three serving in WWII) and appearing in seven World Series. The Dodgers' career WAR leader (66.4) had a keen eye at the plate, but often remarked that he wished he would have swung more.

Reese's .366 on-base percentage outshined his .269 batting average, and despite his laments, is what made him a special player. He only batted over .300 once and never hit more than 16 home runs in a single season, but his walks totals were historic. He owns two of the five total 100-walk seasons for a shortstop in National League history (1947, 104; 1949, 116), and no shortstop in the NL has topped the 100 mark since.

Duke Snider *(OF, 1947–62)*: The Duke is the Dodgers' franchise home run leader, with 389. He hit at least 40 home runs for five straight seasons from 1953–57, and is the only center fielder in NL history to do so.

Snider shined on the big stage too, collecting a .945 OPS in 36 World Series games, with more RBIs (26) and home runs (11) than any other National League player, ever.

Sandy Koufax *(LHP, 1955–66)*: Koufax is well-known for having a too-brief career, but he still played 12 seasons. The late-bloomer was just 54–53 with a 3.94 ERA his first seven seasons—the stretch no one talks about. The next five seasons, he averaged 22 wins, with a 1.95 ERA, in one of the most remarkable runs in the game's history.

During the five-year stretch . . .

- Koufax led the league in wins three times, won three Cy Youngs, one MVP, and took home the ERA title each season. He's the only National Leaguer to win pitching's Triple Crown three times, leading the league in wins, ERA, and strikeouts in the same season (1963, 1965–66), and he's the only NL player to do it twice in a row since Grover Cleveland Alexander did it for the Phillies in 1915–16.

- Was nearly unhittable at Dodger Stadium, going 57–15 with a 1.37 ERA and .176 batting average against.
- Became the only pitcher since 1920 to have four seasons with a sub-2.05 ERA—and he had them all in a row! During that 1963–66 stretch, Koufax maintained a 1.86 ERA. Thirty-five qualifying Hall of Fame pitchers never had an ERA that low in even one single season.

Koufax, over those last two seasons (1965–66), became the last NL hurler since 1904 with consecutive 300+ inning, 300+ strikeout seasons. And then . . . he was done. Just like that.

Despite long stretches of dominance, Koufax was pitching with severe elbow pain, beginning in late 1964. Following the 1966 World Series, Koufax and his ailing elbow had had enough.

Don Drysdale *(RHP, 1956–69)*: Drysdale is, kinda sorta, *Koufax-Light*. That's not an insult to the Hall of Fame right-hander—it's just incredible how the two teammates' careers seemed to match up.

Like Koufax, Drysdale had a slow-*ish* start to his career, going 79–64 with a 3.30 ERA his first six seasons, before finishing his last seven full seasons at 125–98 with a 2.68 ERA.

Also like Koufax, Drysdale had a short period of complete dominance . . . only it was much shorter than that of Koufax.

In 1968, Drysdale had a then-record 58-inning scoreless streak, later broken by Dodger Orel Hershiser in 1988 (59 innings). He pitched six straight shutouts, an MLB record that still stands, as part of a franchise-best 1.37 first-half ERA.

Unfortunately, like his lefty teammate, Drysdale entered the league as a teenager and was out before his thirty-third birthday. It wasn't an elbow, but a chronically sore shoulder that forced Drysdale to call it quits.

Next-Gen Aces

It's only natural, but it's unfair to compare the Dodgers' 2015 1–2 punch in the starting rotation to the all-time greats, Koufax and Drysdale—but only because Clayton Kershaw and Zack Greinke might be lot better.

Clayton Kershaw throwing his second of an MLB-best three complete-game shutouts during the 2015 season (July 23, 2015). (Arturo Pardavila III, CC BY 2.0)

Kershaw, over his last five years, has claimed four ERA titles, three Cy Youngs, and one MVP award—eerily similar to Koufax's tremendous five-year stretch. He has maintained a 2.11 ERA since 2011, and only four pitchers have even had a *single-season* ERA that low this millennium. Over the last 10 years, Kershaw has the best qualifying ERA in the game (2.43), and no one else is within a half-run of him. Greinke, third-best at 3.04, has been a recent revelation.

From July 30, 2013 to May 16, 2014, right-hander Zack Greinke pitched 21 straight starts surrendering two runs or less (earned or unearned)—a Live Ball Era record, by four whole starts. He upped the ante in 2015, going 19–3 with a league-leading 1.66 ERA, 225 ERA+, and 0.844 WHIP. Since 1881, only three pitchers have topped those numbers—Greg Maddux (1995), Pete Alexander (1915), and Walter Johnson (1913).

STATS INCREDIBLE!

5: Home runs by Adrian Gonzalez to start 2015. Gonzalez was the first player in history to club that many through his team's first three games.

4: Consecutive seasons in which Clayton Kershaw led all of baseball in ERA (2011–14). Cy Young led baseball in ERA just twice during his entire career.

165: Maury Wills's record for games played in 1962. He won the MVP that season, batting .299/.347/.373 with 104 stolen bases.

.356/.311: Pitcher Orel Hershiser's batting average in 1993 (.356) was higher than the on-base percentage of the batters against him (.311).

417: Times right-hander Kevin Brown was at a platoon disadvantage in 2003 (facing left-handed batters). He did not allow a home run to any of them.

0: Sandy Koufax tossed a shutout in Game 5 of the 1965 World Series, on three days' rest. He tossed another in Game 7, on two days' rest.

1: Hyun-Jin Ryu was the first Korean-born pitcher to win a postseason game (2013 NLCS).

123: Hits by Steve Garvey with runners on base in 1975, the most in recorded history. Jackie Robinson is second, with 120 in 1949.

.638: Hanley Ramirez's slugging percentage in 2013—highest ever for a shortstop with 300+ plate appearances.

2: Career [qualified] seasons by Clayton Kershaw with at least 10.00 K/9 and a sub-0.900 WHIP. That is as many as every other pitcher in history *combined*.

4: Pitchers in history that have had consecutive qualified sub-0.900 WHIP seasons: Kershaw (2014–15), Greg Maddux (1994–95), Christy Mathewson (1908–09), and Mordecai Brown (1908–09).

4: Total seasons in which Kershaw had a sub-2.30 ERA and at least 230 strikeouts. No pitcher in baseball history had more (Pedro, Walsh, and Waddell also had four). He is just twenty-eight years old in 2016.

3.92: Kershaw's career ERA in starts he did *not* win. John Lackey has a career 3.92 ERA through 2015.

SAN DIEGO PADRES

Est. 1969

Tony Gwynn ranks 55th all-time in at-bats (9,288), 19th in hits (3,141), and 1,370th in strikeouts (434).

The San Diego Padres entered the league in the 1969 expansion, along with the Montreal Expos (Nationals), Seattle Pilots (Brewers), and Kansas City Royals. To date, the team has five division crowns (1984, 1996, 1998, 2005, 2006), and two National League titles (1984, 1998), but is still seeking its first World Series championship.

The Padres are the only team in Major League Baseball to start with five straight sub-.400 winning percentages . . . and actually had six such seasons at the onset. They had four 100-loss seasons in those first six, which is awkward, because their NL West rival, the San Francisco Giants, have had just one such season in their history (and the Giants are 133 years old and went 102 years before hitting that lone 100-loss season in 1985). But, that's enough hate.

There is a ton to love about Padres history, and they haven't always been basement-dwellers. They finished .500 or better eight times over an 11-year stretch, from 1982–92. If that doesn't sound like a big deal, consider: The Pittsburgh Pirates endured 20 straight sub-.500 seasons from 1993–2012, and the Royals finished over .500 just once from 1995–2012. So, being "not bad" can be a pretty good deal.

Two players, Dave Winfield and Tony Gwynn, don the Pads' cap in the Baseball Hall of Fame, and Trevor Hoffman might not be far behind, having saved an NL-record 601 games over an 18-year career spent mostly in San Diego. Plus, the Padres have those sweet camouflage uniforms, and were the first MLB club to regularly honor and appreciate the United States military.

No, it's not a century-old club, rich with old-timey-nicknamed greats, like Babe, Whitey, Lefty, and Shoeless Joe. But the Padres can still lay claim to one of the best in the game's history.

Perhaps more than any other team in baseball, the Padres, historically, are defined by one player. The Padres really are the Club that Gwynn Built. The lifetime Padre was what one may call "OMG great," to put it in modern context—but his game was old school.

Mr. Padre

Gwynn played 20 years, from 1982–2001, and was one of those rare pure hitters that seemingly could have played forever. He actually had a better OPS in his forties (.823, 2000–01; age forty to forty-one) than he did after his first five seasons in the majors (.804, 1982–86, age twenty-two to twenty-six).

He leads a slew of offensive categories for the franchise, and it's not even close. His totals in hits (3,141), singles (2,378), doubles (543), total bases (4,259), extra-base hits (763), and runs scored (1,383) are all more than those tallied by the second- and third-place players combined. And the scope of his greatness extends far beyond just San Diego history.

Gwynn's greatness, in pieces:

- Batted .338 for his career. No other Padre has hit .338 during any one single season.

- Had a .290 batting average over the WORST 162-game stretch of his career.
- Won the batting title in 1987 with a .370 average. If he went an additional 0-for-56, he still would have won the crown.
- Had more games with 4+ hits (45) than games with multiple strikeouts (34). Babe Ruth had 29 games with 4+ hits, along with 239 multi-strikeout games.
- Gwynn (1993–97), and St. Louis Cardinals second baseman Rogers Hornsby (1920–25) are the only players in National League history with five straight seasons batting .350+.
- During a five-year stretch, from 1993–97, Gwynn maintained a .368 batting average (120 Hall of Fame hitters never hit .368 in any one single season).
- Led the 1980s with a .332 batting average, and the 1990s with a .344.
- From 1970 to 1990, six different players had one single season with 150+ hits and less than 20 strikeouts. Gwynn then had six such seasons, consecutive, from 1991–96.
- Gwynn faced Atlanta Braves ace Greg Maddux 107 times, more than any other pitcher. Maddux led the league in ERA (2.84) during the span of Gwynn's career, but Gwynn still batted .415 against him and never struck out.
- Of course, Gwynn never had a .400 season. But over a 179-game span from July 3, 1993 to May 9, 1995, he maintained a .403 average.
- He's remembered for a slightly rotund physique that he developed later in his career, but Gwynn was a great athlete who stole 319 bases in his career. In 1981, he was taken in the 10th round of the NBA Draft, while his Hall of Fame comPadre, Dave Winfield, was a fifth round pick of the 1973 NBA Draft.

A memorial surrounding Tony Gwynn's "Mr. Padre" statue outside Petco Park in 2014. (Flickr DeeJaySD, CC BY-SA)

Dave Winfield

Winfield is the only other Padre Hall of Famer, and even that's a stretch, as most of his best seasons came later, with the New York Yankees. Still, Winny made his mark.

Winfield played his first eight seasons with the Padres, 1973–80, and was a six-foot-six athletic marvel. The University of Minnesota grad was actually drafted by four pro sports leagues in 1973 (MLB, NBA, ABA, NFL), and made his debut late in the season for San Diego. Despite a late start to the decade, Winfield was one of just seven NL players in the 1970s with 100+ home runs and 100+ stolen bases.

Only 154 of his 465 career home runs came with the Padres (205 with the Yankees), but they were enough. No Padre has had more 20+ home run seasons than Winfield (5; 1974, 1977–80).

Trevor Hoffman

The thing with closers is, only the very best seem to get any respect. And the New York Yankees' Mariano Rivera holds just about every relief pitching record there is . . . leaving Trevor Hoffman in the dust. But, while Mariano was the game's best, Hoffman wasn't far behind, and should eventually be the third Padre represented in the Hall of Fame.

Hoffman retired with the MLB career saves record (601), and it still stands as a National League record—by a healthy margin.

Hoffman could have retired five years earlier and he'd still have a 12-save edge over second-place NL finisher John Franco (424). He's one of only three pitchers (Francisco Rodriguez, Craig Kimbrel) with 40 saves in four straight seasons, and he's the only player in baseball history to do it twice. Rivera's best 40-save streak was three years (2003–05).

STATS INCREDIBLE!

.410: Rickey Henderson's team-high on-base percentage for the Padres in 1996, despite having the lowest qualified batting average on the team (.241).

75.3: The percentage of career games in which Tony Gwynn hit safely.

1: April 14, 1986, the only time Gwynn struck out three or more times in his career. Dodgers hurler Bob Welch K'd the Pads' hits leader his first three at-bats in the game.

38: Nate Colbert's single-season home run total in both 1970 and 1972. It would stand as a team record for 24 years (40; Ken Caminiti, 1996). Greg Vaughn owns the current record, with 50 in 1998.

31: Saves in Trevor Hoffman's career in which he struck out every batter he faced. Most all-time.

296: Hoffman's career "perfect save" total. Only Mariano Rivera had more.

2014/2007: Jason Lane was the starting pitcher for the Padres on July 28, 2014. His first big-league start was on August 20, 2007, as the Astros' center fielder.

434: Both the career strikeout total of Tony Gwynn and Mark Reynolds's strikeout total from 2009–10.

56: Tony Gwynn's career-high in stolen bases was 56, as was the career-high of Deion Sanders, Ichiro, and Jose Altuve. That is four more than Barry Bonds's career-best and nine more than Jimmy Rollins.

1,183: Tony Gwynn would have had to end his career on an 0-for-1,183 skid for his career batting average to fall below .300.

69: Times Gwynn batted with men on second and third with two outs during his career. He never struck out.

58: Times Gwynn struck out looking during his final thirteen seasons. He had an idea of what a strike was.

SAN FRANCISCO GIANTS

Est. 1883

In 2004, Barry Bonds reached base safely 376 times. He had just 373 at-bats. No other player in history has had more times safely on base than at-bats. He turned forty that season.

No matter when or where, the Giants, baseball's winningest team, have seemingly always played well.

Established in 1883 as the New York Gothams, the ballclub got the hang of things quickly, topping .500 in just its second pro season (62–50). Their play emulated their new nickname in 1886, as the "Giants" went 85–27, for an all-time franchise-best .759 winning percentage. They only finished second in the National League that year, but they were closing in on the kind of championship success that would eventually help define the franchise.

The Giants won two straight championships in 1888–89, defeating the American Association's best. But just as those aren't counted as official World Series wins (the AL-NL modern World Series began in 1903), it's probably okay to dismiss the next thirteen years in Giants history, before the first World Series, when the team topped the .500 mark just six times and never finished higher than third in the NL standings.

The dawn of the American League at the turn of the century was also a turning of the page for Major League Baseball. The game had two leagues with staying power, and the Giants would prove to be one of its very best teams. In fact, early on, they probably made the New York Yankees jealous.

After hiring John McGraw as manager in 1902, the Giants quickly became the pride of New York. McGraw had such little respect for the upstart American League (with it, the Yankees), that he refused to play the Boston Americans in the 1904 World Series, which feels so . . . Un-American. The club got in line and won its first official Series the following year, beginning a short-term stretch of five straight 90-win seasons, and a long-term run of success that has been much more sky-line bullet train than roller coaster.

All-time ace Christy Mathewson led a Deadball Era staff including fellow Hall of Famers Joe McGinnity and Rube Marquard, putting up team ERA totals that were routinely under 3.00, collectively. Nine times the Giants had a player win the NL ERA crown, or finish runner-up, from 1903 to 1913. From there, Hall of Fame second baseman Frankie Frisch led a new offensive charge for New York that resulted in four straight World Series trips in the 1920s (1921–24), winning two. By 1924, counting the 1904 abstention, the Giants had played in 9 of the 22 total World Series, while their AL-counterpart Yankees had just one win in three trips.

Christy Mathewson, New York Giants, 1912. (Charles M. Conlon)

From then, of course, the two teams switched fates a bit, and World Series appearances were no longer an inevitability for the Giants. They managed just one championship over the next 29 seasons ("That's plenty," say Padres fans), despite Hall of Fame play from guys like Mel Ott, Carl Hubbell, and Johnny Mize. Even with Bobby Thomson's pennant-winning, come-from-behind, "Shot Heard 'Round the World" homer in 1951—before a World Series they LOST—and an all-time great, Willie Mays, leading them back to Series glory in 1954, they weren't long for New York. Their shots may have been heard the world over, but attendance didn't show it.

Mays helped smooth over the transition to San Francisco in 1958, leading the team in WAR each of its first eight West Coast seasons. For 14 years overall, the team never finished below .500. No World Series wins, but also no poor showings. And that was how the Giants would define themselves for decades after—no wins, but no disastrous runs.

Even with the great Barry Bonds destroying home run records, and discovering a beyond-Ruthian dominance in San Fran, all with an upside-down smile on his face, the Giants went 56 years between World Series wins.

Since, they've won every other year since 2010. Yawn. So it goes for the National League's most consistent franchise.

Big 6

There are only a handful of players in this book (Walter Johnson, Babe Ruth, Ty Cobb, Ted Williams, etc.) that deserve, and likely have, their own stats book. At the very least, they should help push this thing to 1,000 pages with their accomplishments. Alas, we have our limits, even if a few of the players we cover seemingly had none. Christy Mathewson was one of them.

(Willie Mays and Barry Bonds, too, but we'll get to them. . . .)

Mathewson's nickname, "Big 6," was a reference to his stature (six-foot-one), and New York City's famous "Big 6" fire engine.

He was one of the greatest players in the game's history, and, by all accounts, one of the greatest human beings.

The two-time Triple Crown winner (1905; 31–9, 1.28 ERA, 206 strikeouts/ 1908; 37–11, 1.43, 259 Ks) won 373 games in his career (third all-time), with a 2.13 ERA (ninth), and a 1.058 WHIP (seventh). During his best five-year stretch (1907–11), he went 139–51 with a microscopic 1.69 ERA. Basically, he put together five straight 2015 Zack Greinke seasons (1.68 ERA). Over that span, he led the league in wins and ERA three times, and strike-outs twice.

Since 1920, only Bob Gibson (1.12 ERA; 1968) has had an ERA lower than what Mathewson maintained over a three-year stretch from 1908–10 (1.50 ERA).

He was also *big* in the postseason, especially in the 1905 World Series. He tossed a record three straight shutouts in the series, leading the Giants to victory. His 28 scoreless World Series innings to start a career are still a major-league record.

Say Hey!

The Say Hey Kid was perhaps the game's greatest all-around talent, and wasted little time getting there. He batted .477 in 149 at-bats in AAA before getting the call-up and winning the Rookie of the Year award for the Giants in 1951 (.274/.356/.472). After a brief call-up by the *United States military*, Mays won the league MVP his next full season, batting .345 with 41 home runs. From there, it seemed there was nothing he couldn't, or didn't, accomplish. He won two MVPs, a batting title, four home run titles, four straight stolen base titles, and was a 20-time All-Star, one shy of Hank Aaron's major-league record. His 660 home runs are now fifth on the all-time list, but, for a brief period until June 10, 1972 (the date Hank Aaron hit no. 649 and pulled away for good), he held the NL home run record.

And then there's everything else:

- He became the NL's first 30/30 player in 1956 (36 home runs, 40 stolen bases). Then, he became the first repeat 30/30 player in 1957 (35 HRs, 38 SBs).
- He had 13 seasons with at least 70 extra-base hits, a major-league record.
- For each season over a 10-year stretch, from 1957–66, Mays finished in the top six in MVP voting, was an All-Star, and a Gold Glove winner.
- Over that same 10-year run, he had a collective .983 OPS—higher than any single-season OPS of Hall of Famer Dave Winfield.
- He's the only player with both a 50-homer season (1955; 51) and a 20+ triples season (1957; 20).
- Over a five-year stretch, from 1954–58, he averaged 38 home runs—two more than the Kansas City Royals' single-season franchise record (36). His 1.019 OPS over that period is higher than any one single-season OPS of Hall of Famer Reggie Jackson.

B. Bonds

No one had more 30/30 (HR/SB) seasons in baseball history than Bonds.

Bobby? Barry? Take your pick. Father (Bobby) and son (Barry) are the only five-time 30/30 members in baseball history. And while, of course, this section is dedicated to the all-time Home Run King (from here, all "Bonds" references will be to Barry), his father had a heck of a career. In the 1970s, only Hall of Famers Willie Stargell (296), Reggie Jackson (292), and Johnny Bench (290) hit more home runs than Bobby (280) hit.

He certainly passed this trait down to his son, as Barry Bonds ended up with an all-time record 762 home runs—586 with the Giants.

Of course, this is common knowledge, along with his much-heralded single-season record (73; 2001), and the alleged steroid-use stench that has, thus far, kept him from Hall of Fame enshrinement. What's left when the basics are peeled away and the asterisks are, in our opinion, fairly set aside, is a fascinating and nuanced career that's a whole lot of fun to look at:

A slender Barry Bonds, 1993. (Jim Accordino)

(Deep breath)

- From August 14, 2001 to September 7, 2004, hit 154 home runs over the span of 442 games. He struck out just 153 times during that same span.
- Had 379 intentional walks to just 377 strikeouts in his final 3,700 career plate appearances.
- Had a .514 on-base percentage during his final 1,000 career games.
- Batted .289/.473/.596 with 99 Rs, 21 2Bs, 39 HRs, 94 RBIs, 5 SBs, and just 66 Ks in his final 162 career games.
- Batted .303/.387/.655 after falling behind 0–2 in the count from 2002–04.

- From 2000–05, batted .338/.533/.779. No other player ever slashed that in a single qualified season. His 240 OPS+ during that span was only ever matched by Babe Ruth in 1920 and Fred Dunlap in 1884.
- Had 334 home runs and 380 stolen bases through 1996. No other player in baseball history eclipsed both of those totals during their *entire* career.
- Batted .471/.700/1.294 during World Series play, the best batting average, on-base, and slugging percentage of any player with at least 30 World Series plate appearances; however, he never won a ring. Pat Burrell on the other hand, who batted .037/.235/.074 on baseball's biggest stage, won two—including one with Barry's Giants.
- From 2001–05, had a .559 on-base percentage. No other player in history ever reached base at such a rate in a single qualified season.

STATS INCREDIBLE!

10: Barry Bonds's MLB record number of seasons with at least 25 home runs and 25 stolen bases. From 1990 to 1998, he had as many 25/25 seasons (in a row) as Willie Mays (5), Hank Aaron (2), and Alex Rodriguez (2) combined.

3: The number of starts in a World Series by Giants aces Christy Mathewson and Madison Bumgarner, under age twenty-six, with 0–1 runs allowed—a major-league record.

30/45: Bobby Bonds was the first MLB player with 30+ home runs and 45+ stolen bases in 1969 (32 HRs, 45 SBs). His son did it 21 years later (33 HRs, 52 SBs; 1990).

9: Mel Ott's seasons with at least 25 home runs and 100 walks. Only Lou Gehrig, Ted Williams, Babe Ruth, and Barry Bonds had more.

1.000: J. T. Snow (.429) and Barry Bonds (.609) are the only teammates in history to combine for a single-season 1.000+ on-base percentage (2004).

2: Grand slams hit by starting pitcher Madison Bumgarner in 2014, the second pitcher ever with two in the same season. Giants catcher, Buster Posey, hit one the same day as Bumgarner, marking the first time in MLB history a pitcher-catcher battery has combined for two salamis.

136: Consecutive multi-strikeout performances to start RHP Tim Lincecum's career, a major-league record.

80: Home runs hit by Barry Bonds, from April 12, 2001 to April 17, 2002, a span of 160 games.

42: From 1992 to 2007, Barry Bonds had one season in which he had a sub-1.000 OPS. It was .9993 in 2006. He turned forty-two that season.

2: From April 25, 1991 to September 26, 2007, Barry Bonds reached base safely 4,516 times in 2,258 games—an average of exactly two times per game.

162.4: Barry Bonds's career WAR. Ken Griffey Jr. and Pete Rose combined for 162.7 WAR, besting Bonds by just 0.3 wins.

232: Barry Bonds's record walk total in 2004. A decade later, in 2014, no player even saw 232 three-ball counts.

2.59%: Madison Bumgarner's career home run percentage per at-bat. He has hit home runs at a greater rate than he has allowed them (2.21%) during his career (through 2015).

GLOSSARY OF STATS AND TERMS

Adjusted ERA (ERA+): ERA adjusted by park factor and for league averages. It helps present a more neutral assessment of the performance of players who benefited or suffered from high-scoring parks and leagues or the opposite.

Adjusted On-Base Percentage Plus Slugging (OPS+): An important modification of On-Base Percentage, which adjusts the OPS to account for the ballpark and the league that the player played in. In addition, the number is "normalized" so that the median is 100, with better-than-average scores above 100. A single-season OPS+ performance of 140 or higher could be considered a Hall of Fame level performance for that season. Its formula is OPS+ = 100*((OBP/lgOBP)+(SLG/lgSLG) -1), with lgOBP and lgSLG representing the league average for that statistic in that year.

At-bats (AB): A sub-category of plate appearances that excludes certain outcomes including, but not limited to, a base on balls or hit by pitch. The number of at-bats is used to calculate batting average and slugging percentage, while the number of plate appearances is used to calculate a batter's on-base percentage (noting the aforementioned exclusions).

Batting Average (BA): The number of hits gotten by a player divided by his number of at-bats. Batting average has long been viewed as the primary measure of a batter's skill, so that the batting title is awarded to the batter with the highest average, rather than to one who scores or drives in the most runs.

Defensive Runs Saved (DRS): A statistic that measures the number of runs a player saved (or cost) his team on defense relative to an average player. The best fielders typically fall into a range of 15–20 for a season, but any positive number is considered above average.

Defensive Wins Above Replacement (dWAR): A defensive measure of wins above replacement, but given only the defensive stats of the player and his position adjustment. Offensive WAR, or oWAR, uses the same value metrics as WAR, but assumes everyone is an average defender.

Earned Run (ER): A run that is ruled by the official scorer to have resulted exclusively from actions by the batting team and not because of errors by the defense. When the fielding team makes an error or passed ball, the scorer is supposed to "reconstruct" the inning assuming that the defensive miscue did not occur. Only runs that would have scored barring the miscue are considered earned; all others are considered to be unearned.

Earned Run Average (ERA): A primary measure of a pitcher's success. It is expressed as an average number of opponents' earned runs scored per notional nine-inning game. Its formula is (ER x 9) / IP.

Extra-Base Hit (EB, EBH, XBH): A hit that goes for more than one base.

Fielding Independent Pitching (FIP): A sabermetric pitching statistic that is philosophically derived from the concept of

Defense-Independent Pitching Statistics (also known as "DIPS"). It's a stat that mirrors ERA but only uses BBs, Ks, and HRs. The formula for FIP is simply: $(13*HR + 3*BB - 2*K)/IP + C$, where C is a constant term that recenters the league-average FIP to match its average ERA. The weights for FIP were derived from the formula for batting linear weights, setting the DIPS events relative to the average value of a ball in play (essentially zeroing out the runs above/below average from BIP).

Fielding Percentage (FP): A common, though limited, measure of fielding effectiveness. Fielding percentage is calculated as chances accepted divided by total chances, and thus measures how effective a fielder is in avoiding errors.

Home Run Percentage (HR%, AB/HR): A way to measure how frequently a batter hits a home run. To calculate, divide the number of plate appearances by the number of home runs hit.

Isolated Power (ISO): A measure of a batter's ability to hit for extra bases. It is the average number of extra bases beyond first per plate appearance. It can be expressed equivalently as follows: ISO = Slugging percentage - Batting average, or ISO = (Total bases - Hits) / AB, or $ISO = (2B + 2*3B + 3*HR) / AB$.

Jaffe WAR Score System (JAWS): developed by sabermetrician Jay Jaffe (first at Baseball Prospectus in 2004) as a means to measure a player's Hall of Fame worthiness by comparing him to the players at his position who are already enshrined, using advanced metrics to account for the wide variations in offensive levels that have occurred throughout the game's history. The stated goal is to improve the Hall of Fame's standards, or at least to maintain them rather than erode them, by admitting players who are at least as good as the average Hall of Famer at the position, using a means via which longevity isn't the sole determinant of worthiness.

On-Base Percentage (OBP, OB%): A measure of how often a batter reaches base. Batters are not credited with reaching base on an error or fielder's choice, and they are not charged with an opportunity if they make a sacrifice bunt. It is approximately equal to Times on base / Plate appearances; its formula is (H + BB + HBP) / (AB + BB + HBP + SF).

On-Base Plus Slugging (OPS): The sum of on-base percentage and slugging percentage.

Per-162 Stats: An attempt to condense each batter's career into a single season's worth of stats. To calculate for a batter, divide his total number of career games played by 162, then divide his career totals by that factor.

Plate Appearances (PA): Every time a batter completes a turn batting, he is credited with a PA. A player is considered to have completed a turn batting when he reaches base safely via a hit, fielder's choice, or an error, is awarded first base via a base on balls, hit by pitch or interference/obstruction (including catcher's interference), or is retired before reaching base. If a turn at the plate is interrupted by an inning ending on a caught stealing or other similar event that prevents the completion of the batter's turn at the plate, then no PA is charged and the batter leads off the following inning with a fresh count. Similarly, if a game ends on a balk, the player who was batting at the time of the balk is not charged with a PA. If a batter is replaced during time at the plate, the count at the time he is replaced is used to determine whether or not he is charged with a PA. For statistical purposes, plate appearances that result in a batter reaching base via obstruction or interference are ignored when calculating OBP.

Qualifying Player: For a player to qualify for league awards and single season records–

Batters:

Prior to 1920, 60% of team games to qualify, rounded to nearest integer:

1920–37, 100 games.

1938–44, AL - 400 ABs, NL - 100 games.

1945–56, 2.6 at-bats per team game. However, from 1951–54, if a player came up short, a player could still qualify for a batting title if they led after the necessary number of hitless at-bats were added to their at-bat total.

1957–present, 3.1 plate appearances per team game. However, after 1967, if a player came up short, a player could still qualify for a batting title if they led after the necessary number of hitless plate appearances were added to their plate appearance total. Case in point . . . Tony Gwynn, in 1996, hit .353 in 498 plate appearances, but tack on an 0-for-4 (needed 4 plate appearances to qualify) and he still reigns at .349. Moreover, Willie McGee won the 1990 NL batting title, despite finishing the season in the American League. He qualified after the necessary number of hitless plate appearances were added.

In 1954, Bobby Avila won the AL batting title. He bested Ted Williams, despite Williams having a higher batting average. By today's standards, Williams would have won the batting crown, but he had so many walks that he did not have enough official at-bats to qualify. This inspired the change to plate appearances, instead of at-bats, as the qualifier shortly thereafter.

Pitchers:

ERA, per 9 starts: one inning pitched per team game played that season, rounded to nearest integer. In most cases, this will require 162 innings pitched.

Win Percentage—Minimum number of decisions is the number of team games that season multiplied by 0.098 rounded up to the nearest integer. Example: 162-game season, 16 decisions.

Quality Start: A game in which the starting pitcher pitches six or more innings and allows three runs or fewer. The implication is that a quality start allows his team a much better than even chance to win the game and is a credit to the starting pitcher, whether he ends up with a win, a loss, or a no-decision for his efforts.

Slash line: The most commonly used short listing of a player's key offensive statistics. In the 1990s, it replaced the former Triple Crown stat usage, as it more aptly describes a player's offensive contributions. A player's batting average is listed first, then OBP, and finally slugging percentage. For instance, R. J. Reynolds hit .288/.354/.344 for the 1990 Pirates; he had a .288 average, .354 OBP, and .344 slugging percentage.

Slugging Percentage (SLG): The number of total bases divided by the number of at-bats. Its formula is ([Singles] + [Doubles x 2] + [Triples x 3] + [Home Runs x 4])/[At-Bats].

Strikeout Percentage (K%, K Rate): A statistic for either a pitcher or a batter. For a pitcher, it represents the number of strikeouts per batter faced. For a batter, it represents how many times he walks or strikes out per plate appearance.

Strikeout-to-Walk Ratio (K/BB, SO/BB): The measure of a pitcher's ability to control pitches, calculated as: strikeouts divided by bases on balls. A pitcher that possesses a great K/BB ratio is usually a dominant power pitcher.

Walks and Hits per Inning Pitched (WHIP): Walks plus hits, all divided by number of innings pitched. It is one of the standard measures of a pitcher's efficacy, noting how well they prevent baserunners. It became prominent in the 1980s and 1990s.

Win Probability Added (WPA): A statistic that attempts to measure a player's contribution to a win by looking at each of the player's plays within a game, and how that player has altered the outcome.

Wins Above Replacement (WAR): An attempt to measure a player's value—expressed in wins—over that which would have been contributed by a fictional "replacement-level player" (essentially a AAA-quality player who can be readily acquired by a team at any time for the league's minimum salary) in the same amount of playing time.

EAR (Effort Above Replacement): New arbitrary stat we invented, akin to participation trophies for the athletically challenged. Still haven't worked out all the kinks.

Most definitions provided by

INDEX

Note: Illustrations and photographs are indicated by page numbers in *italics*.